Curling Capital

Curling Capital

WINNIPEG AND THE ROARIN' GAME, 1876 TO 1988

Morris Mott and John Allardyce

THE UNIVERSITY OF MANITOBA PRESS

© The University of Manitoba Press 1989
Winnipeg, Manitoba R3T 2N2
Printed in Canada

Design by Norman Schmidt

Front jacket/cover photograph: Canadian Mixed Championship, Brandon, 1989.
Manitoba's team members shown: Jeff Stoughton, Lynn Morrow, Karen Fallis (courtesy
Sandy Black).

Jacket/cover photograph of the authors courtesy Kathie Ellwood.

The publication of this volume was assisted by a grant from the Canada Council.

Cataloguing in Publication Data

Mott, Morris Kenneth, 1946–
Curling capital : Winnipeg and the roarin' game,
1876–1988

Includes bibliographical references and index.
ISBN: 0–88755–145–9 (bound); 0–88755–620–5 (pbk.)

1. Curling – Manitoba – Winnipeg – History. I.
Allardyce, John, 1955–. II. Title.
GV845.M688 1989   796.9'6   C89–098087–X

To Laverne Mott, and to fond memories of Ken Mott, Joan and Bill Allardyce

Contents

Photographs

ABBREVIATIONS

MCA Manitoba Curling Association
PAM Provincial Archives of Manitoba
TCM Turners' Curling Museum, Weyburn
WCPI Western Canadian Pictorial Index, University of Winnipeg

1

Wooden rock (courtesy Doug Fowler and Russell Curling Club) *10*
Iron rock (courtesy TCM) *10*
Outdoor curling, 1880s (courtesy PAM) *11*
A.G.B. Bannatyne (courtesy WCPI) *11*
David Young (courtesy PAM) *14*
Alex Brown (courtesy WCPI) *14*
W.N. Kennedy (courtesy WCPI) *14*
S.L. Bedson (courtesy PAM) *15*
Cover, Winnipeg advertising brochure, 1891 (courtesy PAM) *15*
Rock box with rocks (courtesy TCM) *18*
Rock baskets with rocks (courtesy TCM) *18*
Front of a church decorated for curlers' service (courtesy PAM) *19*
Crampit (courtesy TCM) *22*
R.H. "Bob" Dunbar (courtesy WCPI) *22*
Bob Dunbar delivering rock (*Winnipeg Free Press*, January 2, 1909) *23*
T.A. Lockhart using standard delivery (*Brandon Daily Sun*, January 26, 1909) *23*

2

Group of women curlers, ca. 1908 (courtesy WCPI *Tribune* Collection) *30*
Team of women curlers, 1921 (courtesy MCA) *31*
Two straw brooms from different eras (courtesy TCM) *31*
Granite Curling Club, 1970 (courtesy PAM) *36*
W.A. "Bill" Carson (courtesy MCA) *36*
J.W. de C. O'Grady (courtesy WCPI) *37*
C.C. Chisholm (courtesy MCA) *37*
J.P. Robertson (courtesy PAM) *40*
Isaac Pitblado (courtesy MCA) *40*

Acknowledgements

In preparing this volume we have been helped by many people, organizations and institutions. We are grateful for the opportunity to acknowledge their assistance.

Kurt Refvik and Karen Skinner acted as research assistants for several weeks. We were able to benefit from their skills and enthusiasm through grants from the Brandon University Research Fund, the St. Paul's College Research Fund, and the Manitoba Heritage Federation.

The sources on which we relied came primarily from the following archives and libraries: Provincial Archives of Manitoba; Brandon University Archives; Univerity of Manitoba Archives; the Province of Manitoba's Legislative Library; the Brandon University libraries; the University of Manitoba libraries; the City of Winnipeg libraries. The members of staff at these institutions were invariably efficient and courteous.

The officers and staff of the Manitoba Curling Association and the Manitoba Ladies' Curling Association were very cooperative. Moreover, dozens of curlers and former curlers shared their time, memories, opinions and photographs with us. The names of most of these latter people appear in the notes.

A few passages in this volume first appeared elsewhere. We wish to thank the publishers of the *Journal of Sport History* for permission to use again information contained in volume 7, number 3 (winter 1980); the publishers of *The Urban History Review/Review d'histoire urbaine* for permission to publish material found in volume 12, number 2 (October 1983); the publishers of *Horizon Canada* for consent to publish segments from volume 5, number 49 (February 1986); the publishers of the *Canadian Journal of History of Sport/Revue Canadienne de l' histoire des sports*, for permission to use passages that can be found in volume 19, number 1 (May 1988).

A draft of the manuscript was read by Bob Picken and Gerald Friesen. Each of them made very helpful suggestions. The manuscript was prepared for publication in a most efficient manner by the secretarial staff of the Faculty of Arts, Brandon University, and by the staff in the Computer Services unit, Brandon University.

Finally, we thank Raymonde Mott, Shelley Mott, Kenny Mott, and Kathie Ellwood. They were tolerant of the distracted authors of this book, and supportive in countless ways.

Morris Mott and John Allardyce
May 1989

Curling Capital

Introduction

IN THE WINTER OF 1902–03, curlers from Scotland toured North America for the first time. Six rinks captained by Rev. John Kerr played in a number of centres in Canada and the United States. The Scots found every city exhilarating, but they were impressed especially by Winnipeg. "In the annals of curling" there had been "no place like [it]," Kerr wrote after he returned home. "What St. Andrews is to golf, so is Winnipeg to that other royal and ancient game." To him, the prairie city was "the Mecca of curlers."[1]

The Scots reverend did not choose his words precisely. He did not mean that a Winnipeg club had played a role in the early development of curling similar to that played by St. Andrews in golf. Nor did he mean that every true curler was obligated to visit the western Canadian centre in the same way a Moslem was obligated to visit the birthplace of Muhammed. What Kerr was saying in effect was that Winnipeg was curling's leading city, a curling capital.

Kerr and the Scots curlers who accompanied him regarded Winnipeg as a special centre for several reasons. One was the immense popularity of the sport among Winnipeggers, a popularity reflected partly in the number of curlers, but mostly in the attention paid to curling by the media and the general public. Another reason for pointing to Winnipeg as a special city was that it was the headquarters of the Manitoba Branch of the Royal Caledonian Curling Club (RCCC), soon to be re-named the Manitoba Curling Association (MCA). The Manitoba Branch was a large, progressive organization that sponsored and administered with admirable efficiency the world's biggest annual bonspiel. The excellence of the best Winnipeg curlers was another reason Kerr and his companions singled out this city. So was the sheer number of high-calibre players, people who had introduced or mastered new techniques, strategies and pieces of equipment. Finally, Kerr and the other touring Scots were impressed with the size and success of the banquets and other social occasions arranged by the Manitoba Branch and some of the individual Winnipeg clubs.[2]

Kerr and his friends were not the first to mention Winnipeg's special stature in the curling world, and they certainly weren't the last. In 1893, Judge H.W. Cory of St. Paul, Minnesota, said that Winnipeg was "the Mecca of all good curlers." In 1907, a writer in the Ontario Curling Association's annual yearbook noted that Winnipeg was "the great curling ground" of the North American continent. In 1961, an observer from the *Calgary Herald* referred to Winnipeg as the "curling cradle of the nation." In 1984, a writer in *Saturday Night* said that Winnipeg was "a curling-mad city in a curling-mad province." Similar sentiments were voiced time and again over the years especially, but not only, by Winnipeggers themselves.[3]

On most occasions, individuals who mentioned Winnipeg's special standing in the curling world had one or more of the same facts in mind as the Scots in 1903. They might be thinking of the large number of excellent Winnipeg curlers, or the huge crowds that gathered in the city for key matches, or the coverage given to curling by members of the local media, or the size of the annual MCA bonspiel and the marvellous curling that it featured. In the 1970s or 1980s, they might be thinking less of those reasons and more of three others. The first was the reputation that Manitoba curling organizations in general, and Winnipeg members of them in particular, had acquired by this time as hosts of major curling events other than the bonspiel. The second was the important role Winnipeggers had played in establishing national and international curling championships. The third was the way in which Winnipeggers had promoted around the world the attractions of a competitive, serious approach to the sport. The specific time period or context in which speakers or writers made their remarks would cause them to emphasize some aspects of Winnipeg's prominence and ignore others, but they agreed that the city possessed a unique status among curlers.

This unique status was always the product of the skills, enthusiasm and hard work of key individuals. Short biographical sketches of many of these people have been incorporated into this book. They are included partly because they had an impact on curling. The sketches are provided also because historical developments are understood more readily if they are associated with identifiable characters rather than with impersonal forces, and historians should emphasize the former rather than the latter unless serious inaccuracies will result from doing so.[4]

The major themes in this volume are the rise of Winnipeg to world curling prominence late in the nineteenth century and the persistence of that prominence in the twentieth. However, the book is designed to be informative on two other subjects. These are discussed insofar as they can be without losing focus on the main concerns.

The first of the supplementary subjects is the history of curling "on the ice" – the evolution of techniques, equipment, strategies. Students of curling will know that a fair amount has been written on this by Scottish and Canadian authors. However, these writers have concentrated on developments that occurred in Scotland or eastern Canada prior to the twentieth century.[5] This book should add to knowledge on recent trends in the sport, especially those that took place in western Canada.

The second supplementary subject is the social history of Winnipeg and to a lesser extent of Manitoba and the Canadian West. Curling has been unusually popular in this city, province and region. Professional historians have all but ignored this fact.[6] Journalists have been more conscious of it, but they have not made sufficient effort to incorporate the history of curling into the wider social and cultural history of the communities in which the sport was played.[7] This in-depth study of curling in Winnipeg should offer some insight into relationships between the people of the prairies' metropolis and the people of its hinterland, into relationships between and among different classes and ethnic groups, into social relationships between males and females, and into general attitudes, mores and circumstances. Marshall McLuhan once said that games are "a kind of talking to itself on the part of society." They are "translator[s] of experience."[8] By looking closely at curling in Winnipeg, we may discover that through it the people of the city said things that help us understand them.

4

1

Becoming a Curlers' Mecca, 1876 to 1903

Although curling was played occasionally in Winnipeg before the 1870s, in that decade the sport was firmly established in the city. It was introduced by people of British-Protestant, especially Scottish, background who valued the sport and felt obligated to promote it. By early in the twentieth century their bonspiel and their curlers had acquired an unrivalled international reputation.

THE OBJECTIVE IN CURLING is to score more points than the other team. One gains points by throwing stones that stop closer to a target than stones thrown by the opponent, and that remain closer to the target despite the opponent's efforts to move them. Some or all of these goals have been incorporated into games played for thousands of years in many parts of the world. Therefore it would not be accurate to say that the Scots "invented" curling.

Nevertheless, it is true that the Lowland Scots developed curling as we know it. The Scots began curling at least four hundred years ago. Until early in the nineteenth century they played according to local rules that prescribed varying numbers of players per team and shots per player, and suggested or required rinks of assorted lengths, and stones of diverse shapes and sizes. Then, as improved means of transportation made it possible for curlers to compete against distant opponents, uniformity of rules became desirable. This was largely accomplished through the formation in 1838 of the Grand Caledonian Curling Club. This club, which

became the Royal Caledonian Curling Club in 1843 after Prince Albert agreed to become patron, was not so much a club as it was an association of clubs. It adopted or promoted the most important rules that have marked the sport to the present day: only circular stones are used; a team, or "rink," consists of four players; each player has two shots per end; the sheet of ice, or "rink," on which the game occurs is forty-six yards long from "foot-score to foot-score" (hack to hack).[1]

The Scots not only developed the sport of curling, but they also introduced it to other parts of the world, including British North America. By the time the RCCC was formed in the late 1830s, British North Americans had been curling for decades. The first to play the sport in the New World may have been the Scottish soldiers in the British Army, which occupied Quebec over the winter of 1759–60. Curling certainly had been introduced by the late eighteenth century, and the first club on the continent was established in 1807 in Montreal. By 1867, a host of clubs had been formed in the four

British colonies that united in that year to form the Dominion of Canada. Clubs were especially numerous and active in Upper Canada, or what is now eastern, southern and western Ontario.

Especially after the formation of the RCCC, British North Americans attempted to adopt rules and equipment employed in Scotland. However, in some parts of what is now central Canada, granite was not available locally, and to import rocks from Scotland was either impossible or too expensive. Therefore "rocks" might be made of wood or iron, and rules might be adjusted to accommodate the altered equipment. Wooden rocks were commonplace in Upper Canada. They often featured an iron handle, as well as an iron band wrapped around the circumference to prevent splitting. Meanwhile, in Lower Canada, or Quebec, rocks were more often fashioned from iron than from wood. Normally iron rocks were heavier than granites and much heavier than woods. When used indoors, or even when used outside on mild days, the irons had a tendency to dig into the ice, particularly when left stationary for a few minutes. Curlers who threw take-outs with irons were often frustrated because the rock that was hit might not move. The irons did have one positive quality, however. In very cold weather they did not break as easily as granites did.[2]

While some Scots were establishing curling in the settled communities of what are now central and eastern Canada, others were attempting to do so in the West, where the main economic activities were still associated with the fur trade. In November 1839, men from the Hudson's Bay Company curled with "flat stones" (no handles) on the east side of the Rocky Mountains, probably in what is now the United States.[3] Quite likely other traders curled after a fashion at different times thereafter, with equipment made from material close at hand.

Meanwhile, inhabitants of the Red River Settlement also took up curling. The Settlement incorporated approximately the area that became known as Greater Winnipeg. It had been established in 1811–12 by Lord Selkirk and the Hudson's Bay Company, and one of its main purposes was to provide cheap food for the northern traders. It contained about 2,000 people in 1824, about 6,700 in 1856, and close to 12,000 by 1870. Among the earliest and most tenacious settlers were the relatively small number of Scots who built homes over the years, especially in the parishes of St. John's, St. Paul's (Middlechurch), and St. Andrew's. It is not known when the settlers first curled, and it is unlikely they played often.[4] However, it seems certain that they did curl from time to time with wooden rocks on keen patches of ice on rivers and ponds.

This conclusion is suggested especially in a letter from "Templeton," published on March 28, 1860, in the newly founded Settlement newspaper, the *Nor'Wester*. In his letter Templeton described the game of curling as it was played in Scotland, and mentioned that some gentlemen who presumably lived in, or very close to, the tiny village of Winnipeg, located at the middle of the Settlement, planned to form the Royal Fort Garry Curling Club "as soon as possible." These Winnipeggers wanted to arrange games with curlers from the "lower district," which evidently meant St. Andrew's parish.[5] It seems that the Royal Fort Garry Club was never established, but both Templeton's letter and other documents indicate that several people in the Settlement were familiar with curling and participated in it occasionally before Red River became part of the Dominion of Canada in 1870.[6]

It was not until 1876, however, that curling became well established in the city that soon became the leading centre for the sport. In 1870 the Dominion of Canada had acquired the West from the Hudson's Bay

Company and divided it into the small Province of Manitoba and the huge North West Territory. The small village of Winnipeg had been chosen the seat of government for both. Sporadically over the next few years individuals from Winnipeg tried to form a curling club, and they succeeded on November 9, 1876, when the Manitoba Curling Club was established.

The Manitoba Curling Club is usually referred to as the first curling club in the West, but it may not have been. In the winter of 1873–74 construction workers at the federal penitentiary at Stony Mountain had curled with iron rocks in a lumber shed they had converted into a one-sheet rink. Whether they formed a club is not known, but if so, the club was inactive by the late 1870s. The Manitoba Curling Club was really the first club in western Canada to achieve a degree of permanence. It originally had about twenty members. They purchased land from A.G.B. Bannatyne on the western edge of town near the present site of Victoria and Albert School and constructed a rink. In this rink, on December 11, in the afternoon because there were no lights, eight members of the new organization participated in the first club match.[7]

Fewer that twenty-seven years after these unimpressive beginnings, Rev. John Kerr was saying that Winnipeg was the world's leading curling city. To him and to several other curling observers by this time, it was obvious that Winnipeg and Winnipeggers were remarkable.[8] How and why had they become so?

The Manitoba Curling Club that was formed in 1876 quickly became a reasonably healthy organization. However, it was an "iron" club, and some of its members preferred granite stones. In 1881 they broke away to form a new club named, appropriately, the Granite Curling Club. For three seasons the two entities shared the same facilities, but more and more curlers switched to granites, and late in 1883 the iron club folded.[9] From that point forward iron rocks were rarely seen, and by the 1890s the only curlers who did not use granites were the youngsters who often learned the game with wooden blocks or jam pails.[10]

The Granite Club was the only curling club in Winnipeg from 1883 to 1887. In the latter year a majority of members decided to take advantage of the opportunity to move to a better rink than the one they were renting. A minority, some of whom were shareholders in the building the Granite Club was using, disagreed with the choice and they formed a new club, the Thistle Curling Club.[11] Like the Granite, the Thistle is still a thriving club today.

Meanwhile, between 1879 and 1888, a number of clubs were formed in smaller prairie towns and cities such as Emerson, Portage la Prairie, Brandon, Gladstone and others beyond the Manitoba boundary as far west as Calgary.[12] Curlers in these centres, like those in Winnipeg, often started with iron or wooden "stones," but soon discarded them in favour of granites.[13] By the 1890s granites were used almost always.

In these pioneer years almost all curlers in Winnipeg and in the smaller western places were Protestants of British origin or descent: Anglicans, Methodists, Presbyterians or Congregationalists who were English, Irish and especially Scots. Occasionally they were emigrants from the United States, but normally they were from Great Britain or eastern Canada and in particular Ontario. They were members of the British-Protestant community that in the 1870s and 1880s was rapidly becoming the most numerous and most powerful group in Manitoba. By the late 1880s they represented almost two-thirds of the population and had made the province a "British and Canadian" one, to quote the late W.L. Morton. They had made the exportation of grain rather than furs the cornerstone of the economy, and had established their institutions, values and ways of doing things as the dominant ones.[14]

These people enjoyed a remarkable variety of sports and other recreations, and they transferred virtually all of them to Winnipeg and to the West. However, they tended to look for "higher" motives than mere enjoyment for participating in sports or other pastimes. They had been influenced by the idea, rooted in Puritanism but by the mid-nineteenth century diffused widely through British and North American Protestantism, that frivolity had to be guarded against closely.[15] The basis of this notion was that God frowned upon levity, but its widespread influence came from confidence that both national and individual progress resulted from diligence and devotion to duty. The new British-Protestant majority in Winnipeg and Manitoba assumed that the English-speaking peoples had become the most prosperous and progressive in the world because they had been more industrious than others. They assumed also that what separated great people from ordinary or insignificant ones was not talent or fortunate circumstances but determination and the willingness to use leisure for self-improvement. This new majority often referred to "time" as "money," and in general they believed that one's success in this life and fitness for the next depended upon how one "spent" that time.[16]

The prevalence of these beliefs meant that for the early British-Protestant Manitobans, as for the English Evangelicals to whom the following words refer, recreation "had always to be held at arm's length, to be closely scrutinized before being welcomed."[17] The recreations that met with approval seemed to have two qualities: they refreshed the body and mind so that those who played them returned to work with renewed energy; and they were morally instructive, which is to say, they dramatized important truths.[18] Some popular amusements, including cock-fighting, dog-fighting, many card games, and some forms of dancing, were of questionable value because they did not possess these qualities.[19] However, one group of recreations was all but universally acclaimed. These were the sports referred to as "manly."

Manly sports were sports that tested, rewarded and therefore revealed the importance of physical, mental and moral qualities that were considered desirable in the male. Curling was a manly sport.[20] It tested a host of praiseworthy attributes including vigour, endurance, determination, power of concentration, ability to plan strategy and capacity to work with others. This alone made it a highly regarded activity and one that the new British-Protestant majority hoped would flourish in the West.

But there was another reason as well to transfer the sport to the prairies. This was the sense of obligation felt by the new majority to transplant in the West the best features of British, Canadian and "Anglo-Saxon" civilization.[21] In particular they felt duty bound to introduce components of that civilization which could thrive in a cold climate. They assumed with justification that the manly sports in general, and the team sports played with a ball or ball-type object in particular, were more popular among the English-speaking peoples of the world than among others. They believed also that in the bracing winter air of the Canadian West some of the best of those sports, particularly curling, should be played often and played well. All of this suggested to them that Manitoba would not be a truly British and Canadian part of the world until manly sports and especially winter team games such as curling were solidly established.[22]

One indication that curling was considered an important part of the culture being transferred to Winnipeg and the West

8

was that so many prominent citizens were active in establishing the early clubs. These individuals represented the "potent minority" of conscientious "culture bearers" who, in nearly every North American frontier society, have taken the lead in re-creating in a new environment what they consider the most praiseworthy features of the civilization left behind.[23]

Among the people who established curling in Winnipeg, one of the most energetic was the remarkable A.G.B. Bannatyne. Bannatyne was an Orkney man who became an employee of the Hudson's Bay Company in the 1840s. In the 1850s he moved to Red River and became one of the first merchants in the Settlement. In the 1870s and 1880s he was one of Winnipeg's leading entrepreneurs. He was an original member of the Manitoba Curling Club, and took part in its first game on December 11, 1876. Later he served on the Executive Committee of the organization, and as its patron. Over the years he was as well an officer of baseball, cricket, rifling and snowshoeing organizations. He also served as an officer or board member of such non-sporting organizations as the Winnipeg General Hospital; the St. Andrew's Society; the Manitoba Club; Manitoba College (the Presbyterian educational institution); the University of Manitoba; the Winnipeg Ladies' School (a private school for girls); a dancing club called the Ariel Club; the Provincial Agricultural Society; and the Historical and Scientific Society of Manitoba.[24]

Another prominent organizer of curling and other activities was David Young. He was the first president of the Granite Curling Club, and before he assumed that position he had served on the Committee of Management of the Manitoba Curling Club. Young was born in Scotland in 1848 but grew up in Ontario and the United States. He came to the West in 1870 as part of the Wolseley expedition sent out by the Government of Canada to ensure a peaceful transfer of the Hudson's Bay Company territory to the Dominion; he stayed after his discharge to become first an employee and then a partner in the prosperous grain-forwarding and dry-goods firm known by the late 1870s as Higgins, Jackson and Young. Young was an officer of lacrosse, baseball and cricket, as well as curling clubs. He was a director of the Dufferin Park Association, the joint-stock company that built Winnipeg's first athletic stadium. He was also a prominent Mason, treasurer of the Provincial Agricultural Society, and an officer of both the Ariel Club and the Winnipeg Dramatic and Literary Society.[25]

Alex Brown was the first president of the Thistle Curling Club. He had been an original officer of both the Manitoba and Granite clubs before he helped form the Thistle; he also skipped one of the rinks in the famous game of December 11, 1876. He was one of the partners in a thriving lumber firm, Brown and Rutherford. Brown was a Scotsman who had resided in Ontario before coming to Winnipeg in 1872. He was one of the first members of the Winnipeg Board of Trade, a city councillor for three years, one of the early chiefs of Winnipeg's volunteer fire brigade, and a member of the Board of Directors of Knox Presbyterian Church.[26]

Colonel W.N. Kennedy was an original officer of the Manitoba Curling Club, and served on its Committee of Management in three different seasons. Kennedy was an Ontarian who came to Manitoba with Wolseley in 1870. He stayed to become prominent in business and military circles, Winnipeg's second Mayor, and a member of the first Council of the North West Territory. Besides being one of Manitoba's hardest-working Masons, he was a high-ranking officer in such organizations as the Winnipeg Philharmonic Society, the Manitoba Bible Society, an early Winnipeg branch of the YMCA, and the Winnipeg chap-

Iron rock

Wooden rock used in Russell, Manitoba, late in the nineteenth century. The handle and iron band are not original.

Outdoor curling, Asessippi district, 1880s

A.G.B. Bannatyne

ter of the Agricultural and Industrial Society of Manitoba. He served on the Board of Management of Wesley College, the Methodist educational institution incorporated in 1877, as well as on the Protestant section of the Manitoba School Board. In sports, he worked to establish and promote not only curling, but cricket and rifling as well. He was also the first president of the Dufferin Park Association.[27]

Outside Winnipeg, the people who established the early curling clubs also were often prominent individuals active in a host of cultural affairs and institutions. For example, the man who in the early 1880s either founded the Stony Mountain Curling Club or re-established the earlier one was S.L. Bedson. Bedson was an Englishman who emigrated to eastern Canada as a young man and then came west as part of the Wolseley expedition of 1870. He stayed in Manitoba to become warden of the Manitoba Penitentiary, which was located at Lower Fort Garry until 1876 and at Stony Mountain thereafter. He was prominent in trapshooting, snowshoeing and rifling organizations; quite likely he also established at Stony Mountain the first golf course in the province. He was an officer of the St. George's Society, the County of Lisgar Agricultural Society, the Masonic Lodge, and the St. John's College Ladies' School located in Winnipeg.[28]

In other rural Manitoba centres there were people nearly as indefatigable as Bedson was in Stony Mountain. Thomas Wastie in Brandon and John Mason in Gladstone are two who stand out.[29] The individuals who established curling in Winnipeg and the West were the same ones who made sure that institutions associated with several other manly sports, with education, with religion, and with other important matters were founded as well.

Due to the efforts of these early enthusiasts, curling became a popular winter sport in Winnipeg and in other towns and cities on the prairies during the 1880s. As one might expect, the curlers quickly became accustomed to local competition and grew a little tired of it. They visited and hosted each other periodically, and occasionally they travelled from several places to one location for a tournament, or "bonspiel." The largest and most successful of the early, intermittent bonspiels were held in Winnipeg in 1884 and 1887. The curlers who participated in them enjoyed the matches against outsiders. They also enjoyed the receptions that occurred after the games, when "brithers o' the broom" gathered to listen to songs and recitations, to share food and drinks and jokes and cigars, to watch or perform Scottish dances, and to explain to each other why various shots had been missed.[30]

At their gatherings in the early to mid-1880s, as well as in their local clubs, the curlers discussed the possibility of forming an association for the West. It would become an affiliate of the RCCC in Scotland, just as eastern Canadian associations had. Through that affiliation, western curlers would be able to keep in close touch with the parent club of their sport, as well as with world developments in technique, equipment and strategy. More important, through an association, western curlers could hold an annual bonspiel. Such an event would allow them to assemble regularly for fun and good fellowship. It would also provide a means through which western curlers might show that they could play their game as well as anyone, and thereby prove to themselves and to the world that the sport was well entrenched in the region.[31]

After half a dozen years of discussion, on December 6, 1888, representatives of seven Manitoba clubs, the Granite and Thistle clubs from Winnipeg, and the Portage la Prairie, Carberry, Morden, Stonewall and Stony Mountain organizations, met at the request of the Granite Club and formed the Manitoba Branch of the RCCC.[32] They decided that the headquarters would be in Winnipeg. At the time, Winnipeg was the grain-marketing, wholesale-distributing and financial-services metropolis for a hinterland that stretched from Lake Superior to the Rockies. More important, it was the only place that could host a bonspiel like the one the branch hoped to develop. By 1888 the city had well over 20,000 people, and was at least six times larger than any other centre between Ontario and British Columbia.[33] A railway network connected it to virtually every settled district in Manitoba and to most of the West.[34] Winnipeg also possessed an aggressive business community that could be expected to help create an outstanding prize list. For all these reasons, Winnipeg was the obvious choice as base of operations for the new organization.

The Manitoba Branch quickly became one of the largest and most important organizations in the sport. At the end of the first year, 1889, the branch represented fourteen clubs and almost 700 curlers. Five years later, it represented thirty-five clubs and about 1,300 curlers, which probably made it the second-largest curling association in Canada, only the Ontario Curling Association being larger.[35] By 1903, the Manitoba Branch had surpassed in size even the Ontario organization. In this year it had become a network of nearly 3,000 curlers from 97 clubs, stretching from Schreiber, Ontario, to Golden, B.C. Most of the clubs were located in agricultural service centres in rural Manitoba, but the branch represented curlers from a larger geographic area than any other curling association in the world. It continued to do so until 1904, when separate associations were formed in those parts of the North West Territories that were about to become the provinces of Saskatchewan and Alberta.[36]

For curlers in the branch, and even for some in the United States and eastern Canada, Winnipeg quickly became more than the headquarters of an important organization. It was also the site of the bonspiel they wanted to attend at least once, especially if they had a local reputation as "crack" shots. The first Manitoba Branch Bonspiel was held in 1889. A few organizational difficulties marred this 'spiel and the next, but thereafter most of the wrinkles were ironed out. By 1895 or so, a format had been established that made for a very successful event.[37]

In the months leading up to the bonspiel, the secretary of the branch, J.P. Robertson, along with the Executive Committee, made the necessary arrangements. They obtained the prizes, some provided by businesses, others purchased with money that was donated. They arranged for special rates for curlers travelling to and from Winnipeg by rail; at this time virtually all visitors used this means of transportation. They agreed to a contract with a carting company that would be responsible for moving rocks from rink to rink; until the 1930s, curlers owned their own rocks and transported them in wooden boxes. Robertson and the Executive Committee also reserved the skating ice they thought would be required over and above the regular curling ice available through the city's clubs.

By 1895 there were three curling clubs in Winnipeg. In 1892 the Assiniboine Curling Club had been formed primarily by former Granite Club curlers who lived south of the Assiniboine River. They built their own three-sheet facility on Mayfair Avenue.[38] In the same year both the Granite and Thistle clubs had built new rinks that were more solid and more satisfactory than the temporary ones they had occupied over the years; the Granite's new six-sheet facility was located at the corner of Ellice and Hargrave, the Thistle's new four-sheeter was on Alexander Avenue near Main Street.[39] The three 1892 rinks were the only ones in the city for the next decade, and were the main facilities used in the bonspiel.

David Young

W.N. Kennedy

Alex Brown

S.L. Bedson

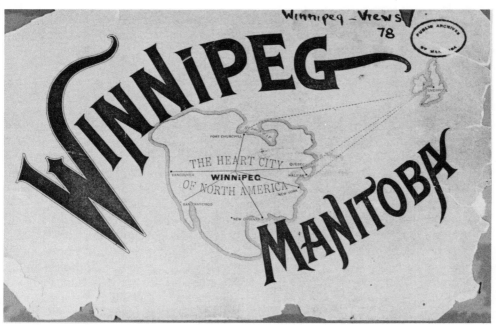

*Cover, Winnipeg advertising brochure,
1891*

In early to mid-February, as the starting date for the bonspiel approached, Robertson received and acknowledged entries in the various events. After 1890, only those teams that had won preliminary district competitions were eligible for certain events; this is one reason the bonspiel featured a large number of very skilled shot-makers. The 'spiel began early in the week, usually on a Monday or a Tuesday, with a short business meeting at headquarters, which was always a major city hotel. Once the meeting was over, the draws were made and the competition began either that same night or the next morning.

From 1891, at some point during the first week of the event, a banquet or smoking concert was arranged by the City of Winnipeg and perhaps the host hotel. The mayor welcomed the visiting curlers and indicated to them that the police had been instructed not to spoil their fun. Then through songs, recitations, toasts and speeches, the curlers confirmed their love of the West and their confidence in its future, their loyalty to Canada and the British Empire, their strong feelings of attachment to their "brithers" from the United States, and their devotion to the roarin' game. Most of them also had a drink or two. The curlers tended to pride themselves on their moderate use of alcoholic beverages, but evidently most of them assumed that wherever there were curlers there would also be whisky. One of their banquet songs, sung to the tune of "Dae yae ken John Peel," went as follows:[40]

My freens I'm gaun tae tell you how,
If you would curl quite right
You must learn to sup on parritch
An' drink hot Scotch at night,
Ye may tak' a dram i' the mornin' too,
But you never maun get tight,
If you want to be a really first class curler.

Chorus:
For the skip may shout elbu' in or elbu' out,

Sandy gie us a gaird here, or knock that deil
out;
But if you chance to make a hog, oh how
they'll roar and shout;
Then hurrah! for the roarin' game o'
curlin'.

The skip he is the maister, awhiles he's on
the rink
And you should do what ere he wants, when
ere he tips the wink,
And if you chance to win an end, you may
go tak' a drink
If you want to be a really first-class curler.

Chorus

When you meet a curler out, why just tip
him the sign,
And take' him doun to the nearest tap and
gie him a sup o' wine,
You should always look on curlers as good
cronies of thine
If you want to be a really first-class curler.

Chorus

From 1894 onward, on the Sunday that fell either before or after the first week's play, the curlers' church service was held. Curlers' services did not originate in Winnipeg, and other bonspiels featured them periodically. In Winnipeg, however, the curlers' service seemed to become a more prominent component of the bonspiel than it did elsewhere. It remained part of the official schedule until early in the 1970s.

The man responsible for instituting the curlers' services at the bonspiels of the Manitoba Branch was Rev. Hugh Pedley of Winnipeg's Central Congregational Church. Pedley became widely known across Canada after he moved to Montreal and became an articulate proponent of the kind of Protestant church union that finally did occur in 1925 with the creation of the United Church of Canada. He was very fond of curling, and was chaplain of Winnipeg's Granite Club from 1892 to 1898, as well as chaplain of the Manitoba Branch from 1894 to 1896 and from 1898 to 1900.[41] When first appointed chaplain of the branch, Pedley felt he should be more than an ornamental officer. He decided that just before the bonspiel opened he would conduct a service in his church in which the sermon would explore the "spiritual significance" of curling. The sermon was given and favourably received.[42] So were similar sermons rendered in each of the next two years. By 1897 the curlers' service had become an institution.

Pedley's sermons, like most of those delivered by the chaplains who succeeded him, examined analogies between the game of curling and the "game" of life. In one of his six bonspiel sermons, Pedley noted similarities between sweeping in curling and helping in life. In another he drew attention to the value of self-control in both curling and life.[43] In his best effort, he compared a host of faulty curling shots and their causes to a number of mistakes made by people every day, and the reasons for the mistakes. Curlers who missed shots because they failed to keep their eyes on the broom were like people who did not succeed in life because they had no definite objective. Curlers who "hogged" their rocks did so either because they lacked "resolution" or because they did not receive enough help from their sweepers; they were like individuals who failed in life either because they were overly cautious or because their friends did not give them timely assistance. Curlers who fired their shots right through the house lacked moderation; they resembled, in the wider world, students who concentrated so much on developing their intellectual capacities that they ruined their health, or men of affairs who devoted so much energy to making money that they lost the desire and the capacity to do good with it. Just as one bad curling shot often ruined a perfectly planned and otherwise perfectly executed end, so one foolish act frequently destroyed an exemplary life. Sometimes curlers failed to guard a good shot; in normal life, human beings sometimes failed to build on their strengths. Curlers who mistakenly guarded an opponent's stone or raised one into the house were like individuals in the wider world who played into the Devil's hands by acting with indifference to corruption and vice, by associating with "vicious" companions, or by "stealthily" reading "ellicit [sic] publications." According to the *Manitoba Free Press*, Pedley concluded his sermon with a marvellous peroration in which he said he

. . . hoped that the curlers would not this week make many of these bad shots; but he still more profoundly hoped that in the great battle of life, the larger arena, the mightier struggle, none of them would do the foolish things that had their counterpart in these bad shots on the ice. He urged them not to forget the spiritual element, but to think of that warfare against sin and evil which every true man is called to wage. And when the fading honour of the bonspiel should be passed, when cup and locket and medal should be gone to rust and decay, might it be theirs to receive the fadeless laurels from the King himself as one who had fought a good fight and left a good record in this world."[44]

The curlers applauded sermons such as Pedley's because he, like other chaplains, was a very capable exponent of a "philosophy" of curling and manly sports. Some of the curlers were inclined to feel guilty about doing nothing more than curl and have fun for a week. The chaplains assured them that curling was a noble recreation. It tested coordination, discipline, calmness under pressure, and other important qualities. Because the sport tested these attributes it revealed their beauty. It also showed that

Rock box with rocks (top)

Rock baskets with rocks, rarely used in Canada (bottom)

Front of a church decorated for curlers'
service, early twentieth century

they were indispensable for success. Accomplishments in a curling match and by extension in life might be enjoyed by those who were lucky. As a rule, however, and as something to be relied upon, they were attained by those who were skilled, morally upright, physically fit and keen-minded.[45] Curling was a ceremony that confirmed the correctness of a certain vision of how the world worked. Through the bonspiel sermons the messages delivered in the ceremony were translated into words.

By early in the second week of the bonspiel, most teams were knocked out of the several events. The more successful teams might compete in semi-finals and finals for two or three more days. The rinks were jammed with hundreds of observers for these matches; in Winnipeg curling was from the 1880s onward an important spectator sport.[46] Then, nearly two weeks after the opening draw, the end of the bonspiel was marked by a closing ceremony at which prizes were distributed. This ceremony was the least satisfying official event of the whole bonspiel, and it was quickly abandoned, because most curlers from outside Winnipeg had already gone home by the time it was held.

By the mid-1890s, then, the Manitoba Branch's Winnipeg Bonspiel was solidly established. The only curling event that could compare with it was the one-day Grand Match held annually in Scotland when the weather cooperated, in which northern rinks played southern ones.[47] However, the MCA Bonspiel became *the* curling event of the world in the four or five years after 1898. In 1897, eighty rinks entered. This was eighteen more than in 1889. In 1898, 101 rinks showed up; and in 1902, 120 did so. In 1903, the year the Scottish curlers visited, an unusually high 171 rinks attended, but the 134 and 135 entries in 1904 and 1905, respectively, showed that attendance had reached a new plateau and would likely climb higher.[48]

This growth is attributable partly to the booming economy of western Canada at the time. A weightier reason for the increased attendance is that in 1899 bonspiel organizers began to offer handsome, often expensive pieces of merchandise as prizes.[49] Cups, lockets and medals didn't disappear; they just became less prevalent than they were at other bonspiels, or than they had been previously at Winnipeg. The most important contributor to expansion was the agreement made in 1898 between the Manitoba Branch and different railway companies to allow all visitors to Winnipeg during a specific period while the bonspiel was in progress to travel on special return fares. The curlers themselves had always been granted special rates. Now their wives, families, other relatives and friends were too.[50] More good curlers, especially from distant towns and cities, began to show up for the event. More theatres and stores started holding "bonspiel specials." Western organizations of various kinds began to schedule meetings or conventions to take advantage of the low fares. Early in the twentieth century a week at the bonspiel was starting to become a mid-winter holiday for all kinds of people from Minnesota to the Saskatchewan River, from the Lakehead to the foothills.

The growing number of visitors to Winnipeg would usually watch some of the curling, because they, like Rev. Kerr of the 1903 Scottish team, were aware that "the finest curlers . . . in the world" competed at the Manitoba Branch's Bonspiel.[51] Most of the top shot-makers came right from the host city. In the 1880s Winnipeg curlers had demonstrated that they were superior to players from the northern United States and from other western Canadian centres; in the same decade they were first embarrassed by one-sided losses to the Ontarians, but then caught and even surpassed the easterners in skill.[52] The results in the first fifteen Manitoba Branch bonspiels (1889 to 1903) confirmed the pre-eminence of Winnipeggers. Twenty-five of the forty-two rinks that won major open events came from the city, as did twelve of the first fifteen "points" event winners (a competition that in effect decided the champion individual curler). At the bonspiel, outsiders such as J.D. Flavelle, a renowned skip from Lindsay, Ontario, or E.J. Rochon of Fort William, G.O. Nettleton of St. Paul or W.H. Sparling of Portage la Prairie often made fine showings. But Winnipeggers such as Mark Fortune, W.G. Fraser, Sam Harstone, W.A. Carson and R.H. Dunbar made better ones.[53]

These top Winnipeg curlers excelled at take-outs in particular. They used them especially when holding a lead in the later ends of a match.[54] They had begun to emphasize take-outs early in the 1890s; Winnipeggers and westerners have been identified with the knock-out game ever since. In accentuating take-outs the Winnipeg curlers had adapted their style to the marvellous curling conditions created by the Winnipeg environment.

Since 1876 Winnipeggers had curled almost always in indoor, though unheated, rinks. In Winnipeg it was normally too cold, too windy or too snowy to enjoy curling outside, which is no doubt why the Red River settlers seldom did so. Indoor rinks had become prevalent in Ontario in the third quarter of the nineteenth century;[55] when Winnipeggers built them, they were following an eastern Canadian, not a Scottish, example. These indoor rinks featured sheets of ice which were made by spreading water over level strips of sand or dirt and allowing the water to freeze. As it happened, in contrast to the water available in some other western Canadian centres, the water used in Winnipeg possessed little alkali. This meant that, by late-nineteenth century standards, sheets of ice in Winnipeg seldom had soft spots or falls. For three or four months a year the indoor rinks in the city contained ice as keen and consistent as one could have.

Because they played indoors on ice that was used for curling and nothing else, Winnipeggers, like most Canadians, used hacks rather than crampits. That is to say, to gain a foot-hold for delivery they used permanent holes in the ice rather than portable iron sheets or bars. Hacks allowed curlers to be much more efficient athletes than did crampits. Hacks enabled them to face the target squarely, whereas crampits invited them to look at it sideways. In particular, hacks made it unnecessary for curlers to throw the rock across the body, a technique frequently necessary with crampits;[56] in curling as in baseball, throwing across the body reduces power and accuracy. The hack, together with the keen, true ice, made the knock-out style more effective in Winnipeg than it could be in places where crampits were used or where the ice was less smooth and consistent. The top city curlers of the 1890s were the first to base their styles of play on these circumstances.

At the same time, these Winnipeg curlers were very capable draw-weight players. The keen, level ice they normally encountered made it possible and frequently necessary to throw quiet weight. They became masters, as did J.D. Flavelle of Ontario and a few others, at throwing the rock so that it slowly turned, or curled, its way to its resting place.

Development of this skill was accommodated by late-nineteenth-century adjustments in the preparation of ice and the shape of the stone. As the game had moved indoors, Canadians had learned to "pebble" the ice. Pebbling was applying a thin coating of hot water to the ice just before play began. The hot water froze almost immediately, and rocks thrown over the new layer did not scrape off the lower layers and make the ice "chippy" or heavy.[57] Furthermore, late in the 1870s J.S. Russell of Toronto had developed a stone that was more satisfac-

Crampit

R.H. "Bob" Dunbar (seated left)

Bob Dunbar delivering rock (top). Compare his delivery to the normal style of the time, revealed here by T.A. Lockhart of Souris (bottom).

tory for indoor play than anything available previously. He had done so by experimenting with the diameter of the concave hollow in the stone's bottom and with the width of the "arras," or riding surface, that surrounded the hollow. His Russell's Improved rocks gave just the right amount of "borrow" on solid ice. In the early 1880s Russell's rocks began to be produced in large numbers in Scotland in the factory owned by T. and A. Kay, which later became Andrew Kay and Co. (Curling Stones) Ltd.[58]

Winnipeggers and better curlers across the country soon learned to use the pebbled ice and the new rocks effectively. One Scotsman who made the trip to Canada in 1903 said that against the top rinks at Winnipeg "long guards are of no use whatever," because opponents simply went around them. In Scotland the in-turn and out-turn were used to neutralize falls, or slopes, in the ice – the curler turned the rock against the fall so that it would hold its line.[59] The better rinks at the Winnipeg Bonspiel used turns not only for this purpose but also to "fade," or "draw," rocks across the ice, to use golf terms. The distance the stones moved across the ice was influenced by sweepers who were much more athletic and efficient than any the Scotsmen had witnessed previously.[60] The Manitoba Branch had rewarded strong sweeping through a rule change implemented in 1898. The point at which sweepers could begin to work on a rock was changed from the "middle score" (which was situated half-way down the ice), to the first "hog-line" (which was located exactly thirty-six feet closer than the "middle score" to the point from which the rock was delivered).[61]

Among the many fine curlers in Winnipeg, the acknowledged master of the equipment and styles of play available by the turn of the century was R.H. "Bob" Dunbar. Dunbar was the first of the Winnipeg curling superstars. He was born in Pictou,

Nova Scotia, in 1860. He came to Winnipeg in the late 1870s. Like many great Winnipeg curlers who came after him, Dunbar was a terrific all-round athlete. He was a prominent competitor in ice-skating and roller-skating races, and he excelled in several track-and-field events. In the late 1880s he was introduced to curling, and in the early 1890s he began to concentrate on it. By then he was working as a bartender in a hotel located near his Thistle Club's headquarters, and in spare hours he used to walk to its rink and work on his game. By 1895 he was the best curler in the West, and by 1901, when he left Winnipeg for St. Paul, he was regarded by virtually all observers as the best shot-maker in the sport. His visits to the Winnipeg Bonspiel over the next few years did nothing to diminish his reputation, although other Winnipeg curlers were considered his equal by about 1905.[62]

Dunbar was one of the Winnipeg curlers who developed and utilized the take-out game. He was also the first to employ effectively the sliding delivery that accommodated that style of play. Quite likely he used a slide because frequently he wanted to throw heavy weight. This required more thrust from the legs than was called for in a light shot, so he learned to bend his knees more and his waist less than curlers previously had. He also learned that his delivery was smoother and that it produced more accurate shots if he allowed his momentum to carry him a short way forward out of the hack.[63] Dunbar thus "discovered" important principles of body mechanics that the majority of top curlers have followed ever since.

By the time Dunbar left the city, a group of younger curlers, led by "Mac" Braden, had learned a great deal from him, either through formal instruction or simply by watching the genius perform. To some extent they copied his delivery and his strategies, but mostly they learned from his attitude. They studied their sport thoroughly and they competed intensely. At the same time, in the tradition of not only Dunbar but also the best eastern Canadian and Scottish curlers, they placed great emphasis on controlling their emotions.

By 1903, then, Winnipeg was the headquarters of a major curling association that was promoting improvements in the game and was sponsoring the world's greatest bonspiel. It was also the home of a number of the finest players in the sport, individuals who were using new equipment and techniques to make the game a better test of manly qualities than it ever had been previously. Winnipeggers could legitimately claim by this time that theirs was the greatest curling city on earth.

2

"Greatest Curling City in the World," 1903 to 1928

In the first quarter of the twentieth century, Winnipeggers began to curl in far greater numbers than they had previously. This represented a new reason to regard Manitoba's capital as the most important city in the sport. However, Winnipeg's reputation as a curling centre was enhanced during these years primarily because of the stability of the MCA, the growing size and success of the association's annual Winnipeg Bonspiel, and the excellence of the city's top curlers.

AT THE TURN OF THE CENTURY, Winnipeg curlers were recognized as exceptionally skilled, but there were surprisingly few participants in the sport at this time. In 1902–03 the three city clubs – the Granite, the Thistle and the Assiniboine – had a total of only a little more than 250 members,[1] and aside from club members very few people seem to have curled.

During the next twenty-five years, this situation changed dramatically. Between 1903 and 1914, when the First World War began, five new clubs were formed: the Civic (1904); the Strathcona–Free Press (1908), which soon became simply the Strathcona; the St. John's (1909); the Elmwood (1911); and the Union-Terminals (1911). They along with the three older organizations made eight clubs, and the eight served a total of over 1,000 members.[2] During the Great War, curling did not decline in popularity as most sports did, because it did not rely on the participation of young men in their physical prime. The

result was that two more clubs were formed by 1918, the Heather (1915), and the Deer Lodge (1918),[3] and by the end of the war the number of members in the ten city clubs was still around 1,000.[4] In the next decade several new clubs were established: the Fort Rouge (1919); the West Kildonan (1919); the Manitoba Agricultural College (ca. 1920); the CPR (1920); the University of Manitoba (ca. 1923); the Telephones (1924); the Eaton (1924); the Fort Garry (1927); the Caledonian (1927); and the Grain Exchange (1928).[5] Meanwhile the Assiniboine and Union-Terminals clubs folded, the former early in the 1920s, and the latter in 1927. Many of the Assiniboine curlers eventually joined the Grain Exchange Club. The Union-Terminals membership had always come mostly from employees of the Canadian Northern and Grand Trunk Pacific Railroad companies; the Fort Garry Club was really a successor to the Union-Terminals, and many Fort Garry members were employees of the

27

Canadian National Railway Company, the company which represented an amalgamation of the Canadian Northern and the Grand Trunk Pacific.[6] By the end of the 1920s the total membership of the nineteen city clubs must have been well over 1,500.[7]

The increase in the number of clubs and members was impressive, but it alone does not reveal the true magnitude of the explosion of participation that occurred early in the twentieth century. More significant was the entrance into the sport by individuals who rented facilities. In the decade before the First World War, corporations, fraternal organizations, trade unions and other entities began to purchase ice from clubs for different periods of time, and sometimes they rented the club members' rocks and brooms as well.[8] Usually the renters arranged for bonspiels that lasted from one to three days. Sometimes they formed a league and used the ice once or twice a week throughout the winter. Between 1903 and 1927, among the many organizations or groups that arranged for sporadic curling were Ashdown's Hardware, Clan Stewart, Knights of Pythias, Winnipeg Fire Department, Winnipeg Caterers' Association, Stovel Company, Sons of Scotland, Manitoba Medical Association, Young Methodist Church, Hudson's Bay Retail, Robinson and Company (Hardware), Masonic lodges, groups of packers, lumbermen, railway workers, school teachers, electrical company employees, telegraphers, travellers, printers and grocers.[9]

The development of casual curling on rented ice and perhaps with rented equipment encouraged broader participation patterns than had existed earlier. Individuals could now enjoy the sport periodically even if they could not afford to spend $25 or $30 on equipment and $5 to $25 annually for a club membership, to use 1911–14 amounts;[10] one must remember that at this time even skilled labourers earned only $20

or $30 per week.[11] Moreover, even the clubs themselves became somewhat more democratic in the new century. Curling had never been an exclusive sport in Winnipeg. Still, in the earlier years most club members had been middle-class or upper-class men. Usually they were businessmen, professional men or white-collar employees with managerial responsibilities; there were few tradesmen, general labourers or other members of the "working" class. Among the 221 members of city clubs in 1891–92 whose occupations can be identifed, twenty-five were from the working class, whereas 196 were from the middle or upper classes. In 1898–99, of 207 identifiable club members, twenty-four were from the working class. Thereafter, more working-class men showed up on club rosters; by 1916–17, eighty-seven of 671 identifiable club members were from the working class.[12] It is not possible to identify large numbers of club members after 1917. However, between 1917 and 1928, clubs were formed in working-class districts such as Fort Rouge and West Kildonan. They were also formed for employees of the CPR, the T. Eaton Company, and Manitoba Telephones. All of this suggests that in the early twentieth century curling actually became what its promoters had prematurely claimed it was – a game for all classes.[13]

Those who are fond of identifying conspiracies in history might want to show that the middle and upper classes of Winnipeg made the game available to the working class in order to control the assumptions and ideas of "inferiors." No such effort is required; there can be no doubt that one reason curling and other manly sports were promoted by men with money and power among those who had fewer resources was to "educate" them on such matters as the necessity of obeying rules and the importance of acquiring certain skills or personality traits.[14] In doing this they acted neither viciously nor surprisingly. They believed that the messages delivered through curling and other sports were both true and important; they wanted others to hear these messages and to benefit from them. They behaved very much like religious people who are confident they know the way to eternal happiness, or like reformers who genuinely believe that if governments implement their plans the world will be a better place. Furthermore, there is no evidence that the middle and upper classes had to impose their ideas on the working class. Construction labourers may have had more respect for physical strength and toughness than did accountants or merchants, but for the most part members of the different classes valued the same manly attributes and felt these should be rewarded in sports and all aspects of life.[15]

Another reason for the increase in number of curlers was that women began to participate in the sport. Until late in the nineteenth century, Winnipeggers had been like most Victorians around the English-speaking world (both men and women) in that they had discouraged females from taking part in sports that required vigour. Engaging in croquet or golf, or in doubles tennis, was acceptable, but participating in more physically demanding sports seemed too likely to cause damage to allegedly frail female bodies.[16] However, early in the new century, Winnipeggers like most Edwardians became convinced that women should possess and demonstrate more vitality, and as a result women's curling was applauded.

One reason a more active woman became acceptable was that in rapidly growing cities such as Winnipeg (which had about 42,000 people in 1901 but 180,000 by 1921), young people seemed physically "softer" than youngsters of previous generations.[17] Because the assumption prevailed that body, mind and soul were interconnected, it was felt that physical weakness would result inevitably in mental

and moral deterioration; in fact, some people argued that the recent growth of juvenile delinquency, transiency and other problems of youth revealed that the process of decay was already under way. Suddenly, raising healthier children became a priority, and it followed that the health of prospective mothers became of immense concern.[18]

Curling was believed to be the perfect sport to develop and dramatize feminine strength and vigour. It required more energy and muscular power than golf, croquet or tennis, but it did not call for body contact, and it provided plenty of opportunity for demonstrating the "feminine" qualities of grace, elegance and modesty. It was a sport through which the new ideal woman, slightly more energetic and hardy than the old, might be realized.[19]

Winnipeg women first began to curl near the end of the first decade of the twentieth century, a few years later than eastern-Canadian or even Scottish women had.[20] Given the common Victorian-Edwardian view that females were more charitable and benevolent than males, it is not surprising that Winnipeg women initially became involved in the sport through "charity bonspiels." Charity bonspiels involved mixed rinks, and as the term implies they were events in which profits from entry fees went to charity. Winnipeg's first charity bonspiel was held in 1908 to raise funds for the newly formed Associated Charities of Winnipeg. The Associated Charities distributed the money to the poor, the sick, the elderly and other unfortunates whose welfare was "naturally" a concern of women.[21]

Later in 1908, the first women's curling club was formed. It was associated with the Granite Club, and had the same administrative structure except that it did not have a chaplain, an officer whom the ladies felt was "only necessary in men's clubs"![22] Within a few years, hundreds of Winnipeg and Manitoba women began to curl. Some

Group of women curlers, ca. 1908

Team of women curlers, 1921

Two straw brooms from different eras, the one on the left popular in the first decades of the century and the one on the right popular in the 1940s and 1950s.

31

did so as leads on men's foursomes, but most did so as members of a growing number of women's clubs, all of which were associated in some way with a men's club.[23] In 1913 the women's clubs were able to arrange for a women's event to be held at the annual MCA Bonspiel, and by the mid-1920s women's events at the bonspiel drew thirty or forty entries. In 1925 the Manitoba Ladies' Curling Association (MLCA) was formed by nine clubs.[24]

In the first quarter of the twentieth century, then, curling became a much more popular participant sport in Winnipeg than it had been earlier. In fact it seems likely that by the mid-1920s there were more curlers in Manitoba's capital than in any other city on earth. Of course these curlers required more and better buildings than they had needed in the nineteenth century, and they acquired those buildings. By this time authorities of the City of Winnipeg, like those of other Canadian urban centres, were beginning to construct and maintain public facilities for the sports dominated by young men and teenage boys. Curling, however, was still a sport that attracted primarily mature men, so the curlers were expected to pay for their own accommodations.

Most of the new clubs built and maintained their own rinks. Usually a group of members formed a property-holding joint-stock company and rented the building to the curling club. The size and location of these facilities can be indicated by referring to those in use in the season of 1925–26.

By this time the Civic Club had a seven-sheet rink on Pacific Avenue East; the club's original location had been on McDermot Avenue just south of the General Hospital, but during the last years of the war the members had rented the old Auditorium Rink (a skating rink) at the corner of York and Garry before they moved to Pacific Avenue in about 1920.[25] In 1925-26 the St. John's Club had their original five-sheet rink at the corner of Machray and Aikins, and the Strathcona had their original five-sheeter just north of Portage Avenue between Furby and Langside.[26] The Elmwood Club's five-sheet rink was at Harbison and Brazier, where their facility always had been and still is.[27] The Union-Terminals Club was, by 1925–26, curling out of a four-sheet rink at 111 Mayfair Avenue that was formerly owned by the Assiniboine Club. The Assiniboine Club had built the structure in 1909, right next door to its 1892 rink, which was torn down. For some reason the Assiniboine Club left the Mayfair Avenue location in 1917–18 and, like the Civic Club, rented ice at the Auditorium Rink. Shortly thereafter the Assiniboine Club disbanded, but the Union-Terminals Club, which had originally curled out of the old Canadian Northern Railway depot at the corner of Main and Water, used the Mayfair Avenue rink until 1927. In that year the Union-Terminals Club folded, and most of the members went to the new Fort Garry Club, which built a six-sheet rink on Main Street at the end of Mayfair. The rink at 111 Mayfair was used by the new Caledonian Club in 1927–28, then by the new Grain Exchange Club when the Caledonian switched to a building at William and Arlington.[28]

The Heather Club's original rink was evidently still in use in the mid–1920s; it was a five-sheeter at Marion and Braemar in St. Boniface. The Deer Lodge's rink had six sheets. It was located at Truro and Bruce in St. James. This was really the second Deer Lodge building – the original club headquarters had been for two years at an open-air rink on Lyle Street. The Fort Rouge Club was still, in the mid-1920s, using its original five-sheet rink at Osborne and Kylemore. The West Kildonan Club's rink was a three-sheeter located on Scotia Street next to the Old Kildonan Cemetary. The Telephones Club had a four-sheet rink at Henry and Gunnell. Evidently at this time the Eaton, CPR, University of Manitoba and

Agricultural College clubs did not have facilities that they could call their own.[29]

The two oldest clubs in the city were using new facilities as well. The Thistle Club replaced its 1892 building with a seven-sheeter constructed in 1912 and located on McDonald Avenue just off Main Street. This rink had to be abandoned when the Thistle Club ran into financial difficulties during the war. The members rented ice at the Auditorium Rink for three or four years, then moved in 1921 to the present Minto Street location.[30] The Granite's new rink was built in 1912–13. It still stands on Mostyn Place, although some alterations have been made to the original structure.

The Granite Club facility soon became the most famous curling rink in the world. The consistent excellence of the top Granite curlers had something to do with this, of course, but so did the attractiveness of the building itself. It cost about $140,000 to construct; this was more than twice the cost of the Thistle Club's 1912 facility, and about ten times the cost of the Fort Rouge Club's 1919 building. Even though the Granite's members were normally well-to-do, it soon became obvious that the club had over-reached itself and could not pay the taxes and the mortgage. In 1916 the Government of Manitoba took over the building and rented it back to the Club for the next thirty years.

The Granite facility was approached through a formal gateway. Constructed primarily of brick and wood, the rink had nine sheets of beautiful ice. In the basement there were lockers and showers. On the main floor were offices and a large open space from which spectators could relax and watch games through windows. On the second floor one found a women's reception room, and a members' lounge with a huge fireplace and heavily upholstered chairs. On the third floor were two billiard tables, a small pool table and card tables.

The *Free Press* once aptly described the rink as a "palace."[31]

Other curling facilities in Winnipeg were not nearly as elaborate as the Granite's. A typical one was built of wood. A person entered it through a door just off a street. The main floor consisted primarily of a large waiting room with windows through which spectators could watch games while sitting on benches or functional chairs. Members' lockers might be at each side of this waiting room, or they might be located in the basement – but the lockers might simply be places to store brooms and hang coats. On a second floor there was likely a club office. Normally there was also a room from which women could watch the games on the ice; even though women were beginning to curl in these years, their primary role in curling, as in other sports, was to cheer for men. The waiting rooms and club rooms were reasonably warm because they contained coal stoves or steam radiators. Out on the ice, of course, the temperature was "regulated . . . by the outside atmosphere."[32]

The sheer growth in the number of Winnipeg curlers, clubs and sheets of ice was one reason the city's reputation as a curling centre was augmented in the early twentieth century. However, when one man said in 1923 that Winnipeg was the "greatest curling city in the world," and when others used phrases that meant effectively the same thing,[33] they were not thinking primarily of numbers of clubs and numbers of members or renters. They were still basing their opinions essentially on the soundness of the MCA, on the size and success of the annual bonspiel sponsored by that organization, and on the level of skill displayed by the city's top shot-makers.

The Manitoba Branch of the Royal Caledonian Curling Club, which in 1908 was re-named the MCA in affiliation with the Royal Caledonian Curling Club, grew stronger and stronger between 1903 and 1928. When the Saskatchewan and Alberta

Curling associations were formed, the number of clubs and curlers in the MCA diminished for a time, of course. However, in curling, as in other economic and social activities in the early twentieth century, as the direct Winnipeg hinterland diminished in size, it increased in density.[34] Over the next two and a half decades, as the population grew steadily on the eastern Canadian prairies and in the northern Great Plains of the United States, and as more people in those regions became familiar with curling, the MCA went from an organization with 103 clubs and about 3,000 members in 1904–05, to one with 137 clubs representing about 4,300 members in 1917–18 and 126 clubs representing over 5,500 members in 1927–28.[35]

As was the case in the late nineteenth century, in the early twentieth century, most of the new clubs and new members were located in the agricultural service centres of southern and western Manitoba. Curling was a popular sport in these communities partly because it was played at a "slow" time of the year. It is also true that curling, like baseball, softball and horseshoes, could be enjoyed by both good athletes and "hackers," mainly because it not only rewards great skill, but it also allows for visiting and joke-telling between shots.[36]

The MCA experienced no major problems during these years. Periodically, representatives of rural clubs complained that Winnipeg curlers were not visiting outside points in sufficient numbers, but the officers of the association and of the Winnipeg clubs responded quickly and constructively to make sure that city curlers and the MCA became more visible in the country.[37] Tensions between parts of the province were definitely present, but they were never serious enough to cause curlers to break away from the provincial body and form their own district associations, as happened in Ontario and Alberta. Moreover, there is no indication that large numbers of rural Manitoba curlers refused to affiliate with their provincial association, as was true of rural curlers in Saskatchewan.[38]

The excellent health of the MCA can be attributed primarily to the dedication and imagination of its main officers. These people were Winnipeggers.[39] Vice-presidents of the association were from clubs located outside the city, but the president, secretary-treasurer and members of the Executive Council came from Winnipeg organizations. Urban people did not necessarily have a special gift for administration; many rural Manitoba curlers could have filled offices just as capably as city ones did. The main reason Winnipeggers were over-represented in the administrative positions of the MCA was that they could conveniently attend meetings as members of the various committees that were required to conduct affairs. They carried out their duties very effectively.

Many early-twentieth-century presidents of the MCA served the curlers of the province with dedication and imagination. One of those who worked hardest was the ebullient W.A. "Bill" Carson, president in 1906–07. Between about 1895 and 1915, Carson was one of the half-dozen best curlers in the world. He threw third rocks for Bob Dunbar in the 1890s. When Dunbar moved to Minnesota, Carson began to skip his own Thistle Club rink, and he did so until he died in a fire in 1920. Like Gordon Hudson, R.J. Gourley, Bruce Hudson and several later MCA officers, Carson had the energy and concentration required to play the game at the highest level while at the same time capably administering it. As MCA president and as an officer of the Thistle Club, he travelled countless miles and spent much of his time and more than a little of his money promoting his sport.[40]

J.W. de C. O'Grady was another early-twentieth-century president who had a particularly positive effect on the MCA and on curling in general. He was an innovator.

34

Unlike Carson, who was the proprietor of a billiard hall and who lived for curling and horse racing, O'Grady was a recreational sportsman who was also a big businessman – a financier – and he was an officer of a number of important organizations, notably the 90th Rifles Battalion. He was one of only three MCA presidents who have served two terms in that office; O'Grady headed the organization in 1907–08 and in 1911–12. During his first term he realized that the MCA would benefit if curlers from member clubs could compete for a trophy offered somewhere other than at the Winnipeg Bonspiel. Accordingly, he put up the O'Grady Challenge Trophy, which would go initially to a club winning a special, "double rink," event at the 1908 bonspiel and which would be thereafter a double-rink challenge cup. Clubs that wanted to challenge for the handsome trophy submitted bids to trustees. The trustees then made sure that the club holding the cup defended it within a reasonable length of time.

The O'Grady Challenge Trophy matches, which still occur today, helped create an immense amount of goodwill between rural and urban curlers. Almost as soon as it was offered, it became the custom for the host club to entertain their visitors as best they could. Winning the games was always important, but having a good time at the banquets and parties afterwards became obligatory. In fact, it was not unknown for the host club to arrange for a "designated drinker" to encourage visiting curlers to get into the "spirit" of the O'Grady before the matches were played.[41]

A third very important president of the MCA was C.C. Chisholm, an architect by profession, who held the office in 1921–22. In 1916, long before he became president, Chisholm made an important contribution to the bonspiel by devising the "Chisholm draw." This draw speeded up play by making it impossible for any one rink to win

prizes in more than two open events; the idea soon caught on across the West. Chisholm's most important act during his year as president was to establish the Honorary Life Members Association. The MCA had selected honorary life members since 1906, and Chisholm knew that some of the wisest and most dedicated curling executives in the province were among those members. He suggested to some of them that they form an association. Chisholm felt the members could help make arrangements for the annual bonspiel, and that they could organize special events for some of the elderly curlers expected to come with the Scottish team that would visit Canada in 1923. The Honorary Life Members Association was formed in February 1922, and it has been an important MCA body ever since. Some people call it the MCA's "senate."[42]

Presidents such as Carson, O'Grady and Chisholm contributed immensely to the welfare of the MCA. However, through most of the quarter century discussed in this chapter, by far the most important individual officer of the organization was J.P. Robertson. At the founding meeting of the Manitoba Branch in December 1888, Robertson had been elected secretary-treasurer on the fourth ballot. For twenty-nine consecutive years thereafter, he was elected to the same position by acclamation. He finally managed to convince the association to accept his resignation in 1918.[43]

Robertson was like many of the early Manitoba curlers, and especially like many officers of the early curling organizations: he had Scottish-Ontario roots, and he became a highly respected citizen who was active in a host of institutions whose purpose was to transfer aspects of British-Ontario culture to the Canadian West. He had been born in the old country in 1841, had come to Ontario with his parents in 1845, and had grown up there to become a teacher and then a journalist. He came to Manitoba

Granite Curling Club, 1970

W.A. "Bill" Carson

J.W. de C. O'Grady

C.C. Chisholm

37

to work for the *Winnipeg Times* in 1879; he soon moved to the *Free Press*. In 1884 he became provincial librarian, and he remained in that position until he died in 1919. The organizations in which he was most active, aside from the MCA, were the Presbyterian Church and the St. Andrew's Society.[44]

It would be impossible to estimate the amount of time Robertson devoted to curling and to the MCA. He was constantly writing or talking to people, offering advice on how to set up clubs, telling officers of existing clubs when he expected to receive their annual reports and membership fees, indicating to individuals from rural communities where they might obtain rocks or brooms for a fair price, finding out what was happening in Scotland or in the East. He compiled annual yearbooks that are truly fascinating documents; because he was provincial librarian a copy of each of them can be found in the rare book room of the Provincial Library of Manitoba. They incorporate minutes of meetings, results of every match in the MCA Bonspiel, complete lists of officers and members of every club in the association, and more. The yearbooks prepared by the secretary-treasurers who succeeded him offer much less information than those he prepared. However, to be fair to the others, it should be added that for several years Robertson was assisted in preparing the annual yearbooks by an extremely capable man, Isaac Pitblado, one of the top lawyers in the city, and that the rising cost of paper at the end of the First World War probably had something to do with the altered size and shape of the MCA's publication after Robertson's tenure.[45]

Robertson's main responsibility was to help the members of five or six committees of the Executive Council arrange for the annual bonspiel. He worked as steadily as a Clydesdale would, and with more efficiency. If it were necessary to pick the one person most responsible for making the MCA Bonspiel the greatest annual event in curling, it was Robertson who would be chosen.

The bonspiel he did so much to establish grew bigger and better during his lifetime, then continued to grow and thrive in the 1920s. In some years there were unusually high numbers of entries, such as in 1912 when Scottish curlers visited for a second time, and 251 rinks were on hand. The general growth of the bonspiel may be indicated by these statistics: in 1904 and 1905 there were a little over 130 rinks entered; ten years later there were about 170; there were only a few more ten years later still, but in the six years between 1920 and 1925 there were more than 200 rinks on four occasions.[46] These numbers refer only to the entries in the regular men's events. After 1915 there was a competition for "veterans" (those sixty years of age and over), and in the mid-1920s the event had twenty or thirty entries. Then there were also the women's events, which drew an additional two or three dozen rinks.[47]

This large number of rinks could never have been accommodated had the Manitoba Branch not introduced some important rule changes prior to 1904. First, the number of "ends" that made up a match was reduced. ("Ends" in curling are the same thing as "innings" in baseball.) In the earliest years of curling in Manitoba, twenty-one ends had constituted a game. In the first Winnipeg bonspiels, sixteen to twenty-one ends were played, but by the turn of the century, as the bonspiel had become bigger, fourteen- and even twelve-end games had been introduced. In 1903–04, another important rule change occurred – the size of the "house" was reduced. (The "house" is the target at which curlers throw their stones.) From the 1870s to 1903, the outside ring of the house had been fourteen feet in diameter, but in the latter year it was reduced to twelve feet, making each curling sheet two feet narrower. This change was designed partly to reward skilled players, but mostly to allow medium- to large-sized buildings to incorporate more sheets of ice. Had the dimensions of the sheet and the number of ends not been reduced already, in certain years between 1904 and 1927, the MCA might have been forced to refuse entries to the bonspiel.[48]

Normally more than half the rinks entered in the bonspiel came from rural Manitoba communities, or from villages, towns and cities outside the province.[49] These outside rinks were composed primarily of business- and professional men. In 1905 there were sixty-five non-Winnipeg rinks at the bonspiel. Of the 260 curlers, 125 can be identified. Almost all were merchants, doctors, lawyers, salesmen, clergymen or people with other middle-class occupations.[50] One can identify thirty-two of the sixty-four individuals in total who came to the 1913 bonspiel from Neepawa, Birtle, Cartwright, Foxwarren, Newdale, Roland, Rapid City, Pipestone and Reston, and twenty-five of these people, or more than seventy-five percent, were business- or professional men.[51] Farmers were not as heavily represented on the non-Winnipeg teams as they were later. Of course, in these years, before the use of automobiles became common, farmers found it difficult to curl regularly even in the local clubs. A detailed study of the Oak River Curling Club between 1900 and 1920 has shown that only about one of three members was a farmer. In this district, as in others, farmers who lived more than four or five miles from town simply were not willing to go out on winter nights and hitch up a team of horses to a sleigh or cutter to travel to and from a curling game.[52]

Small-town curlers came to the bonspiel with the strongest rink they could possibly form, because they knew they would meet some stiff competition. But they came for more than the chance to test their curling ability. They came also to find out about recent business or agricultural developments in the West, to meet with wholesalers, or to do a little shopping. Perhaps above all they came to enjoy themselves, and they had plenty of opportunities to do so. This was especially true at the annual reception for visiting curlers which was still held at a big hotel at the end of the first week or the beginning of the second week of the bonspiel.

These receptions were almost always banquets or smokers, with skits, recitations, songs and displays of ventriloquism, gymnastics, dancing or "the manly art of self-defence"; most of all they featured speeches. The curlers knew as they walked into the function that much of what would be said and done was not to be taken seriously, and they were predisposed to find the joke in whatever was presented. This is one of the reasons they laughed so long and so often.[53]

They laughed in particular when a speaker or performer revealed a truth that applied to one or more members of the audience and which had previously been only dimly perceived. For example, in 1918 they found very amusing some remarks made by "Skip" Herchmer of Fernie, British Columbia. Skip was a son of L.W. Herchmer, the famous commissioner of the North West Mounted Police. Skip said he had waited eighteen years to get to the MCA Bonspiel, where "the cream of the world's curling talent congregated." He suggested that no matter what happened in Winnipeg he wanted to return to Fernie with his reputation as a good curler intact. He also wanted to have a marvellous time but spend as little money as possible. For these reasons he had chosen for his rink a wholesale grocer who would be able to obtain food for a good price, a newspaperman who could "advertise his victories and provide ... alibis" for his defeats, and a railway man who would see that Herchmer "got here and home again without paying a fare."

Isaac Pitblado

J.P. Robertson

Virtually all non-Winnipeg curlers in the audience could have chuckled as they recognized through Herchmer's comments an ignoble side of themselves.[54]

The curlers who came to the city for the bonspiel were accompanied or followed by scores of family members, friends or other visitors to Manitoba's capital. Except during the years from 1918 through 1921, when Canadian railway companies faced financial difficulties, there were special bonspiel rates to and from Winnipeg.[55] Many organizations took advantage of the lower fares to hold meetings, conventions and other functions. In 1916, among the two dozen or more meetings, conferences and other events held during the bonspiel were those sponsored by the Manitoba Horticulture and Forestry Association, a beekeepers' association, a blacksmiths' association, a retail merchants' association, former students of the Manitoba Agricultural College (a reunion), a seed-growers' group, and a poultry association.[56] In addition, in the same year and for about half a dozen years thereafter, a winter carnival occurred in association with the bonspiel. It featured military-band concerts and parades, boxing exhibitions, hockey games, horse races on ice, snowshoe and dog-sled races, lectures, opera and vaudeville shows, motion pictures and other things to see and do.[57] All these attractions brought an estimated 25,000 or 30,000 visitors to Winnipeg by 1918; this was nearly 100 times as many visitors as the bonspiels in the early 1890s had drawn.[58] Since the bonspiel had a very positive effect on the local economy, the City of Winnipeg, businesses in the city, and private citizens all contributed liberally to the fund from which prizes were purchased.[59]

The people who won the most valuable and prestigious of these prizes were usually Winnipeggers. From 1904 to 1914 inclusive, the last eleven points competitions were held at the bonspiel. Members of Winnipeg clubs won nine of them.[60] A grand aggregate trophy for best overall record in the open events was initially offered in 1906. In the first twenty-two years of competition for the trophy, there were twenty-five winning rinks, with one three-way and one two-way tie; eighteen of the twenty-five came from city clubs.[61] In the City vs. All-Comers event, held every year but one from 1903 through 1923, in which a selected group of outside teams played a selected group of Winnipeg units and all scores were added to make a grand total for each side, the City won sixteen times, and the All-Comers won four times.[62] No doubt it was easier for the better Winnipeg curlers than for outsiders to enter the bonspiel regularly. Still, curlers of consequence from hundreds of miles in every direction came to this unofficial world championship, and the statistics support an impression that prevailed inside and outside the city: most of the best curlers in Canada and even the world lived right in Winnipeg.[63]

From about 1905 through 1915, the most renowned of those curlers was D.M. "Mac" Braden of the Thistle and then the Granite Club. Braden was Bob Dunbar's pupil; the student was just becoming a top curler when his tutor left the city. Soon Braden was at the level of Dunbar, who was now living in Minnesota but who normally brought a rink north to the big bonspiel. Braden was never the remarkable shot-maker Dunbar was, and he preferred draw weight to running weight. He was an unusually consistent player, however, and he was the top strategist of his time. He figured out shots as a chess master does moves. In one game he was two down coming home (playing the last end), and when he went to throw his last shot there were no rocks in the house. But his team had two stones placed just in front of the rings. For a few moments he circled the rocks, calculating how to hit one stone, then the other, and have both of them and his shooter end up in the house. Once he had

"Mac" Braden's team, 1906. L to R: F. Roy, lead; W.E. Ellerby, second; F.L. Cassidy, third; D.M. "Mac" Braden, skip.

*Frank Cassidy's team, 1910. L to R: Fred
Barnes, lead; Frank Cassidy, skip; Ed
McKittrick, third; Billy Finlay, second.*

decided upon the ice he would take (the amount of curl to allow for) and the weight he would need, he turned and walked purposefully to the other end of the sheet. As was his custom, he efficiently but unhurriedly cleaned his stone, settled into the hack, and threw. He made the shot to pull out the victory. Long after Braden had left Winnipeg for Vancouver in 1917, Manitoba curlers reminded each other of the way in which he had planned and executed this double-raise and roll. It seemed to reveal so clearly Braden's personality, skill and approach to the game.[64]

Braden often selected for his team some of the best young players in the city, and the person who first challenged and then succeeded him as Winnipeg's curling superstar was a man who once had played for him – Frank Cassidy. Cassidy first became prominent as Braden's third in the years from 1904 to 1908. He skipped his own rink for the next few years, then played five years at third for E.J. Rochon, the old Fort William curler who had moved to Winnipeg. In 1918 Cassidy formed his own rink again, and he stayed at skip until 1924 when he moved to California. He died in that most unlikely location for a curler in 1953.

During the twenty-one years that Cassidy was a top curler he compiled a remarkable bonspiel record. Between 1910 and 1914 he won three of the last five points competitions ever held for individual curlers. While playing either skip or third, he won six grand aggregates and twenty important events. In 1910 he skipped a rink that won forty-three of forty-four games; one could easily make the case that this was the most impressive single performance in the history of the bonspiel.

Until late in the 1920s Cassidy was the only shot-maker to be placed by veteran observers in the same class as Bob Dunbar. His delivery resembled Dunbar's, but seemed an even stronger one. Cassidy's featured balance, rhythm and coordination of remarkable efficiency. Just as Bobby Orr left the impression that he could skate as fast as he wanted, so Cassidy seemed capable of throwing a rock as far as he chose. His momentum took him a few feet farther than Dunbar's; Cassidy stopped moving near the back of the eight-foot ring.[65]

The strongest part of Cassidy's game was his ability to make take-out shots with deadly accuracy. In this, too, he resembled Dunbar. However, unlike his predecessor, Cassidy usually did not throw "big" weight. He preferred to use "hack" weight or even "back-ring" weight, and the shot he really liked to play was the quiet hit-and-roll. When, in 1923, the third contingent of Scottish curlers visited the bonspiel they, like previous touring Scots, were impressed with and victimized by Winnipeggers' knock-out manner of playing. The westerners' "splendid running and rolling game was too much for us," one of them wrote. But by this time the top hitters like Cassidy were unlikely to throw the hard ones that Dunbar and an earlier generation of take-out artists had employed.[66]

When Cassidy left Winnipeg, the best curler in the city and probably the world was Gordon Hudson. Hudson was born in Kenora, Ontario, in 1894. As a youngster, he and his brother, Cliff, were fine natural athletes. For their winter sport they were encouraged to take up curling rather than hockey, partly because their father had been manager of the Kenora Thistles Hockey Club on one of the three trips they made to the East between 1903 and 1907 to challenge for the Stanley Cup, and had been appalled by the way hockey players acted off the ice. Gordon joined the Kenora Curling Club in 1908. This club had been affiliated with the Manitoba Branch ever since 1889, and rinks from it regularly came to the MCA Bonspiel. Gordon Hudson attended his first one in 1910.

In 1914, at the age of twenty, Hudson was the star of the bonspiel because he skipped a group of young Kenora men, including brother Cliff, to a tie for the grand aggregate. Two years later he moved with the rest of the family to Winnipeg, and spent the next two years serving in the First World War. He returned to Winnipeg after the war and became a member of the Strathcona Curling Club. This club already possessed some very good curlers. Once Gordon and Cliff Hudson joined the club it became as strong as any in the city, and soon it became known as the "home of champions."

In the 1920s Gordon Hudson's rinks won three grand aggregates and eleven prestigious events at the bonspiel. During this decade he became acknowledged as the equal of any curler, past or present. His style of play and his delivery were patterned after those of Frank Cassidy. He liked the quiet take-out game, and he used a sliding delivery; however, he slid several feet farther than Cassidy had. After Hudson let the rock go, he went past the tee-line and might not stop until he was in the front of the twelve-foot ring. He was able to slide this far because he turned his left ankle so that only the side of his front shoe was in contact with the ice.

An excellent shot-maker and tactician, Hudson was an even better sportsman. It is likely that no other Winnipeg athlete has been liked and respected as much as he was by teammates and opponents alike. He was the easiest skip to play for, and could convince all members of his rink that they were curling a fine game. If a shot or two were missed, Hudson would take the blame for not reading the ice properly, or for giving the sweepers the wrong instructions. People who curled with Hudson for a few games began to believe they could play the sport well! While he instilled confidence in his own men, he also made sure his opponents had every opportunity to show what they could do. He refused to take advantage of "burned" rocks; that is, he gave the other team a chance to re-throw stones that a sweeper had inadvertently touched with a broom or kicked. He made every effort to delay matches if opponents' rocks were not the right temperature. Since curlers owned their own rocks and either moved them themselves or had them transported from rink to rink, the stones could be left in hot or cold places, and then might not act consistently on the ice until they warmed up or cooled down. At the bonspiel, when he played country teams who were not familiar with the peculiar qualities of the ice they were using, he might tell the opposing skip how much weight was required to make a particular shot on this sheet, or indicate where a little "fall" or a "run" was located. Then, at the end of the game, both his voice and his eyes informed members of the other team that he had enjoyed competing against such fine players and such good fellows.[67]

Gordon Hudson was a special curler and a special human being. It was appropriate that he, the best curler of the day, should be the first Winnipegger to skip a rink in the MacDonald Brier, the Dominion championship curling event established in 1927. His rinks were the first of many Brier teams which, over the next thirty years, confirmed the excellence of Winnipeg curlers and revealed to all Canadians just how far Manitobans had taken the ancient Scottish sport.

3

Confirmation of Superiority, 1928 to 1957

In 1927, the W.C. MacDonald Tobacco Company of Montreal, acting on a suggestion made by Winnipeggers, began to sponsor a Canadian championship curling event they named the Brier. This event soon became recognized as the unofficial world championship competition in the sport.[1] The winning rink was regarded as the world's best curling team, just as the club that wins the World Series is viewed as the world's best baseball team. Manitobans, and Winnipeggers in particular, now had a chance to provide undeniable proof of their superiority at the roarin' game, and they did not waste the opportunity. They dominated the event until the middle of the 1950s. For thirty years after the Brier was inaugurated, the rink representing Manitoba was the team to beat, and that rink almost always came from Winnipeg. As a result, Winnipeg's reputation as a curling capital was enhanced. However, that reputation also depended upon the continuing stability of the MCA, and especially upon the success of the annual bonspiel and other events run by that organization.

THE MEN MOST INSTRUMENTAL in establishing a Canadian curling championship event were Winnipeggers or former Winnipeggers. The key person was George J. Cameron.[2] Cameron was born in Ontario and came west in 1900 when still in his teens. For three years he worked for a railway company. In 1903 he joined W.L. Mackenzie Company Limited, and in 1920 he became owner of it. His Winnipeg-based company was the western representative for the W.C. MacDonald Tobacco Company of Montreal.

Once established in Winnipeg, Cameron took up curling. He joined the Thistle Club in 1904, and later became a member of the Strathcona and Granite clubs. He loved the game. One day in 1924, while talking to Walter F. Payne, who was news editor of the *Manitoba Free Press*, a past-president of the MCA as well as one of the founders of the Strathcona Club, Cameron suggested that it would be good for the sport and good for the country if eastern and western Canadian curlers could compete against each other. Payne agreed enthusiastically. Another

George J. Cameron

Walter F. Payne

Peter Lyall

John T. Haig

Winnipegger who liked the idea was John T. Haig, MLA, a former MCA president and co-founder of the Strathcona Club.

As a result of the encouragement he received, Cameron made a special trip to the East to discuss his idea with Walter Stewart, a curling member of the family who owned the MacDonald Company. Stewart was receptive to the argument that eastern and western curlers should get to know each other better. He may also have felt that curlers from the Montreal area would benefit from the opportunity to see that granite stones were superior to iron ones. Accordingly, Stewart agreed that in 1925 the MacDonald Company would sponsor an all-expenses-paid tour of the East for a rink winning a special event at the Winnipeg Bonspiel. The winner also would take home the MacDonald Brier trophy, named after a MacDonald's product.

Both the event at the bonspiel and the eastern tour by the winning rink were a success. One consequence was that George Cameron and Walter Payne were convinced that a Canadian championship bonspiel was possible. Another was that MacDonald's Tobacco decided to sponsor similar arrangements the next year. While travelling through the east with the 1926 Brier event winners from Winnipeg, Cameron discussed his idea with individuals who possessed enough influence to establish a national championship. One of these people was Peter Lyall of Montreal, member of a prominent eastern Canadian construction family. He had lived in Winnipeg for several years prior to the First World War and had become an enthusiastic curler. Another was Thomas Rennie, president of the Ontario Curling Association, who convened the meeting at the Granite Curling Club in Toronto where definite plans for a championship tournament were made.

The organizers agreed that, beginning in 1927, a round-robin competition would occur among rinks representing different parts of the country. The event would take place in Toronto, the city that was easiest to reach for all teams. The MacDonald Tobacco Company would be approached to become sponsor. Walter Stewart agreed to the request, and decided that as part of the sponsoring effort the company would present the MacDonald Brier Tankard to the winning rink. The company appointed three trustees to arrange the event: John T. Haig, Peter Lyall and Thomas Rennie. Later the company decided to offer British Consols trophies to rinks that had earned the right to go to the Brier. In Manitoba the Consols Trophy replaced the original Brier Trophy.[3]

In the first year, 1927, eight rinks representing cities or towns gathered to compete for the tankard. Only one of them came from the West. It was skipped by O.S. Barkwell of Yellow Grass, Saskatchewan, who won the right to go east by beating Alberta and Manitoba champions in a series held in Winnipeg.[4] The next year, largely due to George Cameron's insistence, all three prairie provinces had representatives in the competition. They joined rinks from Northern Ontario, Ontario, Quebec, New Brunswick, Nova Scotia, Toronto and Montreal. From 1932 on, only provincial or territorial rinks have appeared at the Brier, although an "extra" Ontario rink from Northern Ontario has always been present. In 1936 the tournament began to involve teams from coast to coast, when British Columbia sent a representative. A team from Prince Edward Island first competed in the same year; one from Newfoundland in 1951; and one from the Yukon and Northwest Territories in 1975.[5]

In the late 1920s, then, Winnipeggers and former Winnipeggers were among those who worked hardest to establish the Brier. A few years later, in 1940, people from Winnipeg showed the country that the Brier could be a great spectator event.

From 1927 through 1939, inclusive, the Brier was held in Toronto, on the artificial ice of Toronto's Granite Club. However, the notion that the event should be moved from city to city had been present at least as far back as 1929.[6] In 1939 the trustees announced that the next year Winnipeg would host the event.

One of the main reasons Winnipeg was chosen as the location for the first Brier held outside Toronto was that in 1939, when the decision was made, Manitoba rinks had won eight of the first twelve championships. A second reason, however, was that the MCA would be in charge of local arrangements, and the MCA and its member clubs from Winnipeg were regarded as exceptionally capable hosts. The successful smokers and banquets held over the years at the bonspiel partly explain their reputation, as do the extra efforts they made to ensure the comfort of touring Scots curlers. In 1923, for example, two delegates from the MCA met the Scots in Fort William and brought with them a representative of the Royal Alexandra Hotel to distribute room keys and to tag baggage in advance, so that when the visitors arrived in Winnipeg they would not experience the kind of delay in a hotel lobby that they had faced elsewhere.[7] A further reason to regard the MCA and Winnipeg clubs as fine hosts was the success of the receptions and luncheons they had arranged in the 1930s for the rinks representing Saskatchewan, Alberta and British Columbia when these teams stopped in the city on their way east for Brier events.[8]

Beyond the reputation Manitobans had as curlers and as hosts, there was an additional incentive to give Winnipeg the opportunity to hold the 1940 Brier tournament: a large number of spectators could be expected to watch the games. There were three reasons to feel confident about this. First, Winnipeg had an artificial-ice arena, the Amphitheatre, located just off Osborne Street across from the Legislative Buildings. It was essentially a hockey arena; the ice surface in it, as in most arenas, could be troublesome, but the Amphitheatre could accommodate a great many spectators and had facilitated important games in the bonspiel since 1936.[9]

Second, Winnipeggers and other Manitobans loved to watch good curling. Over the years they had flocked by the hundreds and even the thousands to see matches involving shot-makers of reputation. Often the club rinks in which these games occurred could not accommodate all the people who wanted to gain admittance.[10] This is one reason the MCA had decided in the mid-1930s to use the Amphitheatre for the final days of the bonspiel.

The third reason was that the newspapers in the city would treat the event as a major one and give it extensive coverage.[11] Winnipeg papers had paid a great deal of attention to curling since late in the nineteenth century. They did so especially during the bonspiel, of course, but even during the rest of the winter the city's papers included much information on local and world developments in the roarin' game. In the first full week of January 1910, for example, the three Winnipeg dailies devoted 600 inches, or 1.5 percent of the total space available, to curling. In the same week the Toronto dailies allocated 167 inches of space, or .23 percent of their total, to the sport. In the first full week of January 1930, the two Winnipeg dailies used 436 inches for curling, which represented .8 percent of the space in their papers, whereas the Toronto dailies used 142 inches, or .1 percent, of their space. In both years the newspapers in Regina and Edmonton came closer than those in Toronto to meeting the Winnipeg standard of curling coverage, but even they did not match it.[12]

The newspapers in Winnipeg had had for many years sportswriters and sports editors who loved curling and covered it as they would any major sport. Bruce Boreham wrote about curling for the *Telegram* from 1910 to 1912 and then for a short time after

Winnipeg Amphitheatre, 1912

Bruce Boreham

the First World War. In 1920 his newspaper was absorbed by the *Tribune*, and Boreham covered curling for this Southam paper for the next eight years. Boreham was a close friend of George Cameron. He helped Cameron establish the Brier and wrote the first press release on the championship. He quit sportswriting in 1928 to become public relations director for the Canadian National Railways, but for more than forty years he attended the Brier and kept semi-official histories of each year's play that have been collected into one volume, *The Story of "The Brier,"* which represents the most thorough history of any major Canadian sporting event.[13] Before Boreham left the *Tribune*, Johnny Buss had joined the newspaper. Buss was an outgoing, hard-drinking man who enjoyed all sports and the company of all sportsmen. He especially liked the people involved in curling, and from 1932 until 1955 when he died, Buss either covered the sport himself or, as sports editor, made sure it was covered capably by someone else.[14]

Meanwhile at the *Free Press* between 1908 and 1924, W.J. "Billy" Finlay wrote many of the curling items. Finlay was one of the world's most enthusiastic and skilled curlers. He left Winnipeg in 1924 for Vancouver and the *Sun*, and a young Scots printer at the *Free Press* named George Harper asked if he could write the curling stories for the sports pages. Harper soon became the most famous and most important writer on curling in the country. In the winters he spent most of his working hours and much of his spare time in the rinks of Winnipeg and rural Manitoba. He did more for curling than did any other journalist of his time. When the Canadian Curling Reporters formed their association in 1971, they named their annual award for the best curling story the Scotty Harper Memorial Award.[15]

There were many good reasons, then, to believe that a Brier in Winnipeg would be a significant spectator event. And in 1940 it was. The final draw, featuring a match between the Alberta and Manitoba representatives to determine the Canadian champion, was witnessed by nearly 4,000 people. Four other draws were viewed by crowds of 1,000 or more, and about 10,000 people in total watched the competition. In Toronto Briers, a crowd of 300 or 400 per draw had been considered large. C.S. Richardson of Toronto, secretary of the Brier Trustees, could hardly believe what he saw on the final day. According to the *Vancouver Sun*, visitors from across the country were "simply astounded" at the number of observers throughout the week and at their enthusiasm.[16]

The crowds were drawn to the Amphitheatre partly because the calibre of play was exceptional and partly because the Winnipeg rink representing Manitoba never lost a game. However, it's also true that the MCA organizers accommodated the interests of the spectators, and made sure they were entertained, in ways that Brier observers never had been previously. The organizers revealed to the country what had to be done and what would be done when you moved curling from a small facility to a large one. For the most part they implemented practices that had been introduced already for curling at the Amphitheatre during the bonspiel.[17]

In 1940, for the first time in Brier history, the curlers all used neutral, matched stones. The stones had coloured handles, making it easier to tell from a distance just which rocks belonged to which team. For the first time also the rings were painted, which gave spectators a better opportunity to pick out the shot rock, the second shot, the biters and so on. Finally, for the first time an elaborate closing ceremony was arranged, one that featured a marching pipe band. Peter Lyall was present on the final day. He saw the pipe band and the presentations and the enormous crowd carried away by the whole occasion. In his opinion it was "the greatest spectacle in the history of curling."[18]

Over the next few years Brier organizers in Quebec City (1942), Saskatoon (1946), Calgary (1948) and then other centres built on what had occurred in Winnipeg. They especially added a big opening ceremony, and reports or even live broadcasts on national radio.[19] By the 1950s they had created perhaps the only truly national championship event in Canadian sports, because by then the whole country followed the Brier and, unlike the Grey Cup or the Stanley Cup, representatives of every part of the country participated.

During the years the Brier was becoming an important Canadian sports institution, Manitobans, and particularly Winnipeggers, excelled on the ice. Twenty-eight Briers were held between 1927 and 1957; travel restrictions during the Second World War made it impossible to hold the event in 1943, 1944 and 1945. Rinks from the keystone province won fifteen of the twenty-eight Briers, and thirteen of those fifteen winners came from Winnipeg clubs. Over the same period, Alberta rinks won six championships, and no other province could boast of winning the event more than twice. Statistics relating to overall winning percentage also indicate the superiority of Manitobans. They won 80.7 percent of the Brier matches they played from 1927 through 1957. British Columbia rinks had the next best winning percentage, 65.6.[20]

Actually, Manitobans and Winnipeggers were even more prominent in the Brier than these statistics indicate, because almost every year, it seemed, men who had learned to curl in the keystone province or its major city showed up representing other provinces. Howard Palmer, for example, was part of four Alberta Brier representatives in the 1930s and 1940s, and skipped one of them to victory. He had learned to curl in Winnipeg.[21] Ken Weldon was the skip of the Quebec rink in the Briers of 1952, 1953 and

1957. He was born in Winnipeg and began to curl there.[22] The same was true of his third man in 1952 and 1953, Ches McCance, a football player for the Winnipeg Blue Bombers and then the Montreal Alouettes, who took up curling as a second sport while still in Winnipeg.[23] Grant Watson was one of the top curlers in Winnipeg when he moved to the Lakehead in 1951. In 1953 he skipped the Northern Ontario representative at the Brier held that year in Sudbury.[24]

The province most often represented by curlers from Manitoba, other than Manitoba itself, was British Columbia, whose rinks performed much better than most people realize. In 1946 Frank Avery, whose home town was Austin, and in 1952 and 1954 Elwyn "Bung" Cartmell, formerly of Glenboro, went to the Brier with Vancouver Curling Club teams that were composed entirely of Manitobans.[25] Before he skipped the 1946 team, Avery had thrown third rocks on three previous B.C. rinks, and two of them had been skipped by Rolly David, formerly of Deloraine.[26] The most noteworthy former Manitoban who represented B.C. was W.J. "Billy" Finlay. Finlay was born in Orillia, Ontario, in 1888, and he moved to Winnipeg about 1904. He became sports editor of the *Manitoba Free Press* in 1908. He remained in that position for sixteen years, then moved to Vancouver. Finlay was another top curler who was a fine all-round athlete. He was a professional lacrosse player for a time before the First World War, when field lacrosse was one of Manitoba's most popular spectator sports. He became a prominent Winnipeg curler in 1906 when he joined W.A. Carson's Thistle Club rink. By 1909 he was Frank Cassidy's second, and he was on the 1910 Cassidy rink that had such a magnificent bonspiel record. Later he joined the Strathcona Club, formed his own team, and skipped two grand-aggregate winners at the Winnipeg Bonspiel. He was a great curler, though he

Johnny Buss

G.M. "Scotty" Harper (right) on Scotty Harper Night

*Brier teams and officials in front of Fort
Garry Hotel, 1940*

was past his prime when he skipped the B.C. representatives in 1938, 1940 and 1941.[27]

What explains the dominance of the Brier by Manitobans and especially Winnipeggers from the late 1920s to the late 1950s? Their superiority resulted to some extent of course from living in a climate conducive to the development of good curlers. Curling was essentially a natural-ice sport until the 1950s, and prairie curlers had an advantage over British Columbians, Maritimers or central Canadians, except for the few who had access to artificial ice. But how does one account for the ascendancy of Manitobans and particularly Winnipeggers over curlers from northern Ontario or the other prairie provinces?

A reason sometimes cited is one that has been mentioned – the water used in Winnipeg for making ice possessed little salt or alkali. These substances affected ice in Saskatchewan in particular, which meant that curlers from the wheat province had to learn to play heavy weight and had difficulty adjusting to keen natural ice or the artificial ice used for the Brier.[28] This may be part of the explanation. It should not be relied upon too much, however. It may well be that only specific Brier teams from Saskatchewan, rather than Saskatchewan curlers in general, favoured heavy weight;[29] furthermore, some Winnipeg champions were not afraid to throw hard ones down the ice. It seems likely that a more important advantage the better Winnipeg curlers had over their counterparts from rural Manitoba from the rest of the prairies, and even from the rest of the country, was that they faced keen competition all winter long from other top curlers in their own city.

There were always fifteen to twenty Winnipeg teams capable of winning a Canadian championship. They curled against each other frequently. They might meet in regular club games; certainly this was true at the Strathcona Club, in which the "A" group always contained seven or eight of the best two dozen teams in the world.[30] The top Winnipeg rinks might meet each other as well in the Tucker City Championship event, held from 1900 until after the Second World War, a single knock-out event which was a tougher test of curling consistency than the Brier because one could not afford to have even a single bad game.[31] Finally, the better Winnipeg rinks would likely compete against each other at the MCA Bonspiel. By the time a Winnipeg team arrived at the Brier, its members had been confronted with the necessity of making every shot imaginable. They had protected leads. They had come from behind. They had been forced to struggle to victory even if one member of the rink was off his game. They had faced every form of strategy an opponent might throw at them. In short, they were better prepared than other rinks, technically, tactically and psychologically, for whatever developed during the Brier week.[32]

In the thirty years after 1927 the Winnipeg skips who led rinks to a Brier championship comprised most of curling's superstars, and they were athletic heroes in their home city.[33] Too few Canadians recognize their names. Their anonymity is explained in large part by two related facts. First, curling has not been a major sport in the important central Canadian media centres. Second, there has been a tendency to underestimate the athletic prowess of superior curlers. A few years ago *Maclean's* columnist Allan Fotheringham suggested that curlers are not really athletes because "curling is not a sport – any more than golf is." A sport, he said, must require "some running around, some visible exertion."[34] This is a statement with which sports historians and sociologists would disagree.[35] They would acknowledge that curling does not test certain qualities – speed, for example, or toughness. But, except in very minor ways, soccer does not test ability to throw, and the fifty-yard dash does not test

58

endurance. Every sport rewards some qualities and fails to reward others. Curling primarily requires coordination, concentration and capacity to relax no matter how crucial the situation; to a lesser degree it requires stamina and strength as well. It rewards many of the qualities needed by a good golfer or baseball pitcher. The Winnipeg curling superstars of the 1930s, 1940s and 1950s were the best in the *world* at their sport. Their accomplishments deserve as much respect as those of, say, Sam Snead or "Lefty" Gomez.

The first of these superstars was Gordon Hudson. His teams won the Brier in 1928 and 1929. In 1928 his rink finished in a three-way tie with the representatives from Ontario and Alberta, and Hudson won a special round-robin playoff that evidently was arranged on the spot. In 1929 his team was the first to go undefeated through the competition.

Hudson was extremely popular in Toronto for the same reasons he was popular in the West. He also opened many easterners' eyes to just how well the game was played in Winnipeg and on the prairies. He did so not only by making some marvellous shots, but by adopting a strategy that had been used in Winnipeg for at least a decade, but which was unfamiliar to most easterners. In one of the 1928 games he purposely blanked an end rather than draw into the house for a single point. When he did this, it took the Toronto spectators a few moments to understand what they had just seen and to appreciate its significance. Hudson, like other top western skips, often preferred to keep last rock if he could not score more than one point. This meant that unlike most curlers he actually expected to make his last shot whenever he needed to do so![36]

Howard Wood was a second Winnipeg curling superstar. He skipped the team that won the right to tour the East in 1925. The record that his team compiled on their trip, as well as the one achieved by the George Sherwood St. John's Club rink that made the 1926 tour, suggested that Manitoba rinks were a few shots better than those from Ontario and Quebec.[37] Wood went on to skip rinks to victory in the 1930 and 1940 Briers, and in the latter year his team was undefeated in the competition.

Howard Wood was born in Winnipeg in 1888. He was an outstanding athlete as a young man, excelling especially in soccer. He and his three brothers were encouraged to take up curling by their father, D.D. Wood, a member of the Thistle Club and president of the MCA in 1900–01 when it was still called the Manitoba Branch. Howard joined the Thistle Club in 1907 and curled in his first Winnipeg Bonspiel in 1908. He became a prominent competitive curler in the years from 1910 through 1915 while playing for Bill Carson and Mac Braden. In 1915-16 he began to skip his own rink. Three years earlier he and the whole Braden team had moved from the Thistle to the Granite Club, and Wood stayed with the Granite until he died in 1978.

Wood had a truly remarkable career. He was on teams that won seven grand aggregates and fifty-four trophies at the bonspiel. He skipped rinks to victory in two Briers. He threw third rocks on another Brier-winning team in 1932, and he would have skipped the Manitoba representative in the 1945 Brier had the event not been cancelled. He may not have been the greatest curler of them all, but he was a great curler for a longer time than anyone else. He was a tough man to beat at any level of play until he was in his sixties and known as "Pappy."

Wood was a fierce competitor, to use no stronger adjective, and one opposing skip said the "intensity of his concentration" during a match almost caused the air to vibrate. He could play the knock-out game when it was called for, as he did "without mercy" according to the *Edmonton Bulletin* when he was protecting a lead in a game during the 1940 Brier. However, he preferred the draw style of play that suited his straight-from-the-hack delivery. C.H. "Charlie" Scrymgeour played on many teams that curled against Wood. "Howard played a beautiful game," says Scrymgeour, noting that Wood especially liked to use the outside of the house to build up large ends. "You began to see how beautiful it was," continues Scrymgeour, "at about the same time you realized he had you in a hell of a hole."[38]

R.J. "Bob" Gourley skipped Winnipeg's fourth straight Brier-winning rink in 1931. He was born in Peel County, Ontario, in 1878, and moved to Manitoba with his family while still a boy. As a young man he was employed by the Union Bank, and for a decade or so he was transferred from town to town around the prairies. He came to Winnipeg in 1906, and became president of the Beaver Lumber Company and a director of a number of important business firms. He began to curl in Birtle, Manitoba, as a youngster, and he curled everywhere he went with the Union Bank. When he moved to Winnipeg he joined the Granite Club, but then helped form the Strathcona Club in 1908. He was still a member of the Strathcona when he died in 1976.

Gourley was a distinguished-looking, soft-spoken man. Gordon Hudson's son, Bruce, who became a very prominent Winnipeg curler himself, remembers losing a key game in a bonspiel in the 1950s. Gourley had watched the match. When Hudson came off the ice the two men exchanged greetings. Then Gourley mentioned the turning point in the game, a shot in which Hudson had missed a difficult take-out. "I was hoping," Gourley said, "that you would play the draw instead of the take-out in the seventh end." Gourley was saying in effect that any fool could see that the draw was the better alternative. He had a gentle, even delicate way of putting across his ideas.

Gourley's style of play was as quiet as his manner of speaking. Like Wood, he played light weight for the most part, and he hardly slid at all when he delivered his rock. He was the top strategist of his time, and for this reason he often reminded observers of Mac Braden. Gourley was a very easy man to play for, and that was one reason his teams won two grand aggregates at the Winnipeg Bonspiel, plus over a dozen important events. He was also a cracker-jack administrator, as one might expect of a man with his experience in business. He was president of the MCA in 1931, the year he won the Brier, and both before and after that year he was an important member of MCA and Strathcona club committees.[39]

Jim Congalton would have skipped the first Manitoba rink in the Brier had he been able to beat O.S. Barkwell of Saskatchewan in the 1927 western playoff. As it happened, he had to wait until 1930 before he appeared in the Canadian championship. He was Howard Wood's third man in that year. In 1932 he skipped the fifth straight Winnipeg winner of the Tankard. Because his third man, J.M. Campbell, could not go to Toronto due to the serious illness of his father, Howard Wood substituted and played third for Congalton.

Congalton was from Guelph, Ontario. He learned to curl and to play a very solid game of baseball before moving to Winnipeg in 1905 in his mid-twenties. He probably did his best curling as the second on Mac Braden's Thistle Club and then Granite Club rinks from 1912 through 1914. Braden's teams won the grand aggregate at the bonspiel in two of those three years, and in 1939 Gordon Hudson said that the best second he had ever seen was Jimmy Congalton in 1912. However, Congalton was very capable at third or skip, as his two Brier appearances suggest.[40]

Leo Johnson was a smartly-dressed, cigar-smoking, outgoing man who skipped the Manitoba Brier winner in 1934, going undefeated in the process. He also skipped the Manitoba rink which finished the round-robin games in the 1946 Brier tied with two other teams for the lead, but which then lost out in the playoff matches. Moreover, had there been a Brier in 1944, Leo Johnson's rink would have been in it. He also skipped rinks that won two grand aggregates and a host of open events in the bonspiel.

Johnson was born in Winnipeg and as a young man acquired a reputation as a good baseball player. He started to curl with the Deer Lodge Club in 1919 but joined the Strathcona Club in 1926 and stayed there until he died in 1976. He was an exponent of the knock-out game, and he frequently played heavy weight. However, like every great curler, he could make all the shots. That he could draw with the best if he had to was shown in the 1946 Brier, in the eleventh end of his playoff loss to Alberta, when he kept his team in the game with a draw to the four-foot ring to cut his opponents out of a four-ender.

Johnson could be a showman on the ice. For this reason Jack Matheson, who covered curling for the *Winnipeg Tribune* for many years after the Second World War, once suggested that he was an early version of Matt Baldwin of Alberta. Johnson played confidently, even arrogantly. His delivery featured a lengthy slide with his left arm held unusually high. He irritated some spectators, but he was appreciated by both teammates and opponents. They liked him because he had both a bubbly personality and the ability to laugh at himself. They also respected his hard work in administrative positions for both the Strathcona Club and the MCA.[41]

Ken Watson was known as "Mr. Curler" by the 1960s. There are many reasons he became the individual most identified with the sport. He devoted innumerable hours to the promotion of both international and high-school curling. He produced and directed a film, "Magic in Curling," which won an award at the Cannes Film Festival in 1956. He wrote instructional columns in newspapers, as well as four books. Moreover, he was a dedicated administrator at the club, provincial and national levels.

Above all else, Watson was a marvellous player. He skipped the 1936, 1942 and 1949 Brier winners, and his teams lost a total of only two games in the three competitions. He might have skipped another Brier winner in 1943 had the event been held, for his rink earned the right to represent the province. His teams won a record seven grand aggregates at the Winnipeg Bonspiel. Six of these came in succession, from 1942 through 1947. From 1942 through 1949 at the bonspiel his rink won 139 games and lost only thirteen! There can be no doubt that in the 1940s Ken Watson was the best curler in the world, and it would not be difficult to support the argument that he was the finest curler in history.

Watson was born in Minnedosa in 1904 but moved with his family to Winnipeg in 1912. In the 1920s he began to teach school. He joined Crown Life in 1944 and stayed there until he retired in 1983, just three years before he died. He began to curl in earnest early in the 1920s. At first he belonged to the St. John's Club, but in 1931 he joined the Strathcona Club and he remained there until he stopped curling competitively.

He was an extremely keen student of the game. While learning to curl as a young man, he and his friends used to watch Gordon Hudson at every opportunity. "We . . . imitated his mannerisms and his gestures," he later wrote. "But his slide we couldn't imitate. . . . Our ankles weren't strong enough to support a 'side-of-the-foot' or 'heel' delivery." Then late one night, by accident, they discovered that the sliding delivery came easily if you removed your toe rubber from the front foot and slid on the

Brier winners, 1928. L to R: Bill Grant, lead; Ron Singbusch, second; Sam Penwarden, third; Gordon Hudson, skip.

Brier winners, 1929. L to R: Gordon Hudson, skip; Don Rollo, third; Ron Singbusch, second; Bill Grant, lead.

Brier winners, 1930. L to R: Lionel Wood, lead; Victor Wood, second; Jimmy Congalton, third; Howard Wood, skip.

Brier winners, 1940. L to R: Roy Enman, lead; Howard Wood, Jr., second; Ernie Pollard, third; Howard Wood, Sr., skip.

*Brier winners, 1931. L to R: Ray Stewart,
lead; Arnold Lockerbie, second; Ernie Pollard, third; R.J. Gourley, skip.*

*Brier winners, 1932. L to R: Jimmy Con-
galton, skip; Howard Wood, third; Bill
Noble, second; Harry Mawhinney, lead.*

Brier winners, 1934. L to R: Marno
Frederickson, lead; Linc Johnson, second;
Lorne Stewart, third; Leo Johnson, skip.

Brier winners, 1936. L to R standing:
Grant Watson, third; Charlie Kerr, lead;
Marvin MacIntyre, second; seated, Ken
Watson, skip.

sole of a leather shoe. Eureka! They "could slide even further than the Great Gordon Hudson."

With this delivery, a curler could not only slide a long way, but could maintain balance while doing so. The slide enabled you to get your head behind your extended arm so that aiming at the broom was like "sighting down a gun barrel." Watson and his friends worked on the sliding delivery for the next few years and by the early 1930s he and his brother Grant had perfected it. They usually let the rock go at about the time they hit the tee-line, as the rules in force at the Brier required, but their slide carried them beyond the house perhaps as far as the hog-line.

The sliding delivery created a good deal of controversy. Some older curlers felt that long sliders had two unfair advantages. First, they were closer to the target than short sliders when delivering the stone, and they could even guide the rock through falls in the ice that might exist near the end from which they were throwing. Second, long sliders could ride the rock over to one side of the ice before they threw it, thus in effect moving the hack out of the middle of the sheet. The second objection could not stand scrutiny, as Watson himself pointed out. Any curler who rode his rock out of the hack and then pushed it could never hit the broom consistently. The first criticism may have had some validity, but like the second it could be countered by the observation that the direction the rock will take is essentially determined before the curler leaves the hack. Watson believed that "the basic ingredients of any smooth, well coordinated delivery" are the same. Those ingredients are good balance, proper grip, clear vision of the target and relaxed muscles. The long slide represented follow-through, said Watson. Using it was an advantage only insofar as it made it easier to master the essential components of a sound swing delivery.

The long "Winnipeg slide," as it came to be known, was athletically demanding. It was also aesthetically pleasing. Both these qualities made it attractive to the young men who in the 1940s and 1950s were beginning to curl in much greater numbers than previously. Soon a host of strong, supple youths were sliding out to the hog-line and beyond. In 1952 a rule was instituted, for national competitions at least, which required the rock to be delivered from the centre of the sheet. In 1955 another rule prohibited sliding over the hog-line.

Most of the young curlers who were learning to slide of course had never seen Watson. But they may have read his best and most famous book, or at least talked to others who had done so. *Ken Watson on Curling*, published in 1950, is a landmark in the sport. It features clear, concise prose that makes transparent Watson's enthusiasm for the roarin' game, and it sold over 150,000 copies. Young curlers who have wanted to master their sport have studied it ever since, in the same way that ambitious young baseball players later studied Ted Williams's *The Science of Hitting*. Through Watson's book they could learn how to deliver a rock, and much more. They could learn how and why and when to sweep, and how to shape the corn broom so that it became an efficient sweeping instrument. They could learn much about "Strategy in Skipping" and "The Psychology of Team Play," to cite the titles of two chapters. They could learn also why the quiet take-out style of play, pioneered by Frank Cassidy and others of his generation, then mastered by Ken Watson, is the most reliable style at the competitive level.[42]

Jimmy Welsh was another Winnipeg curling superstar of the 1930s, 1940s and 1950s. He was born in Scotland but started curling in the Winnipeg suburb of St. James in 1926 at the age of sixteen. He remained active at the Deer Lodge Club until he died in 1988. He skipped the rink that won the

Brier without a loss in 1947, as well as the rink that represented Manitoba in 1937 and 1954. He also played third on the Johnny Douglas team that carried Manitoba's colours in 1933. He was part of teams that curled in eight British Consols finals, the same number as Ken Watson did. His record at the MCA Bonspiel was only slightly less sparkling than Watson's. Welsh skipped three grand-aggregate winners. Between 1933 and 1942 his teams won 171 of 201 games. In 1937 his foursome won thirty-three of thirty-four games, a performance nearly on a par with that of the Cassidy rink in 1910. He was still winning major events at the bonspiel in the mid-1950s.

Welsh's teams played the heaviest weight of all the top Winnipeg rinks, but Jimmy himself could make beautiful draw shots when necessary. He had a medium-length slide which brought him to a stop near the button. He was very highly regarded by those who played against him. One veteran recalls that Welsh and his whole team carried their excellence with an unpretentiousness that was unusual even in a sport whose top athletes are often modest about their accomplishments. Another opponent remembers Welsh's uncompromising dedication to fair play. To document his point he referred to a bonspiel in the 1950s when the MCA draw-makers inadvertently scheduled his team for a game against Welsh's on the same sheet of ice on which Welsh had curled his previous match. Welsh went far out of his way to have the game moved so that his own team would not be at an advantage. Old-time curlers occasionally pay Welsh the highest tribute a curler of his generation could receive: they compare both his skill and his integrity to Gordon Hudson's.[43]

Bill Walsh skipped Winnipeg rinks to victory in the Briers of 1952 and 1956. To win the latter event he had to make what once was called "the greatest shot in Brier history"; many observers would say now that the greatest shot was the incredible double take-out that Al Hackner of Northern Ontario pulled off in 1985 to tie Pat Ryan of Alberta. Walsh had to use his last rock in an extra end to come around a guard and tap back a stone owned by Alf Phillips of Ontario. Walsh had the luxury of knowing he could hit and roll out and still be tied. He played the quiet take-out weight that was his strength and which seemed to flow naturally from his personality. His rock knocked the Phillips counter out of the house and then stopped rolling at the edge of the twelve-foot ring, chalking up the victory.

Walsh was born in 1917 in Haileybury, Ontario, but moved with his parents to Winnipeg when he was still an infant. He joined the Fort Rouge Curling Club in 1932. He was a dedicated member and administrator of that club until 1971 when he died of cancer. His curling career was interrupted by service in the Second World War. He was with the Royal Winnipeg Rifles, and won two medals for bravery. His bonspiel record did not match those of the other superstars already mentioned. He did not have the chance to curl for as many years as Welsh and Watson and others did, nor was he as consistently brilliant as they were. But when he had his chance at the brass ring, he grabbed it.[44]

Between 1927 and 1957 almost every top curler in Canada had some connection with Winnipeg. This was true of Cliff Manahan, for example, who skipped five Alberta Brier representatives and won the event on two occasions. He learned the skills of curling in Fort William where he was born, but he himself said that he learned to curl competitively at the MCA Bonspiel. In the early 1920s before he moved to Edmonton, Manahan used to come to the bonspiel regularly as the third on the strong Fort William teams skipped by J.G. Macdonald.[45] Even more influenced by the curlers in Winnipeg was Ab Gowanlock, the

67

*Brier winners, 1942. L to R: Jimmy Grant,
lead; Charlie Scrymgeour, second; Grant
Watson, third; Ken Watson, skip.*

*Brier winners, 1949. L to R: Ken Watson,
skip; Grant Watson, third; Lyle Dyker, second; Charlie Read, lead.*

Brier winners, 1947. L to R: Harry Monk, lead; Jock Reid, second; Alex Welsh, third; Jimmy Welsh, skip.

*Brier winners, 1952. L to R: Bill Walsh,
skip; Al Langlois, third; Andy McWilliams,
second; John Watson, lead.*

*Brier winners, 1956. L to R: Bill Walsh,
skip; Al Langlois, third; Cy White, second;
Andy McWilliams, lead.*

Brier winners, 1938. L to R: Bill McKnight, second; Elwyn "Bung" Cartmell, third; Ab Gowanlock, skip; E.R. "Tommie" McKnight, lead.

Brier winners, 1953. L to R: Ab Gowanlock, skip; Jim Williams, third; Art Pollon, second; Russ Jackman, lead.

rural Manitoba curling superstar of the 1930s, 1940s and 1950s.

Gowanlock was born in 1900 and started to curl in Glenboro at the age of sixteen. Had it not been for an injury, he might have devoted his energy to hockey. The Glenboro Curling Club already had some very skilled players by the time Gowanlock became a member. Once he and his generation of curlers built up an enviable record, it was sometimes said that Glenboro had produced more good curlers per capita than any place on earth.

No doubt Gowanlock benefitted from growing up in a strong club, and from competing in one through much of his career. There were all kinds of rural curlers who could sweep efficiently and who had sound deliveries. Some of them came into Winnipeg as young men to further their education or to find employment and stayed in the city to become part of a top Winnipeg rink: Charlie Kerr and Lyle Dyker from different Ken Watson teams are two men who did this. But curlers from rural clubs normally could not find the competition they required to be psychologically and strategically prepared to win a grand aggregate, a British Consols event or a Brier. Ab Gowanlock was an exception. He skipped teams that won four grand aggregates and more than a dozen events at the MCA Bonspiel. He also skipped two of the three rinks from outside Greater Winnipeg that represented Manitoba at the Brier between 1927 and 1957. He won the Canadian championship both times. His first victory came in 1938 when he headed a team from Glenboro that went undefeated. His second victory came in 1953 with a rink from Dauphin, where his job with the provincial Department of Highways had taken him early in the 1940s after short stays in Winnipeg and Brandon, and where he resided until he passed away in 1988.

Gowanlock was extremely popular with curlers and curling spectators in the city.

When his Glenboro rink won the right to represent the province in 1938, Winnipeggers were overjoyed. They had seen him come close to winning on two previous occasions. They knew he had been especially unfortunate in 1935, when he lost his semifinal game because a "hail-Mary" shot by Roy Pritchard of Killarney, who eventually won the Consols event, accidentally moved a guard into the middle of the house. Winnipeggers and Manitobans knew Gowanlock as a handsome, skilled shot-maker who curled very well under pressure and who was as fine a man to play against as could be found.[46]

Skips are always the focus of attention in curling. So they were in the years when Manitobans and especially Winnipeggers dominated the Brier. But the success of the Manitoba rinks depended in large part upon the fine play of the men at third and on the front ends.

Probably the finest third man in the world in the 1930s and 1940s was Grant Watson, Ken's brother. He was on all three Watson teams that won the Brier championship, and on all seven that won the grand aggregate. In the early 1950s he skipped his own rink for a few years. His team won the grand aggregate at the bonspiel in 1951, then he moved to the Lakehead and skipped the Brier representative from Northern Ontario in 1953. He didn't look forward to throwing the last rock as much as Ken did, but no shot was too difficult for him, and he was probably a better strategist than his brother was.[47]

Alex Welsh was a very fine third as well. He was with his brother, Jimmy, from 1947 through the 1950s; in the 1930s and early 1940s he curled with another strong Deer Lodge skip, Hughie Macdonald, and he also had his own rink for a while. Alex Welsh participated in three Briers, in 1933 as second man on Johnny Douglas's rink, and in 1947 and 1954 with his brother. He was a consistent player. The Welsh brothers, like the Watsons, could have switched positions and not lost very much of their effectiveness.[48]

Ab Gowanlock had two very good thirds on his top rinks. Bung Cartmell was on the Glenboro rinks that Gowanlock regularly brought to the bonspiel, and on the 1938 Brier winner. A top third man had to be able to help his team avoid a disastrous end by executing a shot that knocked two or three rocks away from the front of the house in order to make the four-foot ring available for his skip; Ken Watson said that Cartmell and Grant Watson were the best in the game at doing this. Once Gowanlock left Glenboro, Cartmell skipped his own highly competitive teams for about ten years, then moved to B.C. and skipped two B.C. rinks in the Brier. He was a colourful, happy man, the life of many parties. He drank too heavily sometimes, and his streaks of truly brilliant or incredibly horrible shot-making were related to the amounts of alcohol he consumed. He was a much different curler from Jim Williams, who was the third on Gowanlock's 1953 Dauphin Curling Club Brier-winning team. Williams was a sobre and subdued man, and a consistently solid player.[49]

Three more thirds of the 1930s, 1940s and 1950s stand out. Ernie Pollard was with R.J. Gourley in 1931 and with Howard Wood in 1940. He was especially brilliant in 1940.[50] Al Langlois was with Bill Walsh on both the 1952 and 1956 Brier winners, and in the former year he made several particularly key shots.[51] Lorne Stewart was a top-notch shot-maker. He proved it in 1934 with Leo Johnson's Brier championship rink. He did not do so in 1951 with Roy Forsyth's fourth-place finisher.[52]

From the 1920s through the 1950s the two men who curled at the front-end positions, lead and second, were expected to be enthusiastic sweepers. As shot-makers, the leads were supposed to excel at draws or guards, the seconds at hits.[53] There were many fine leads and seconds in Manitoba in the years under consideration here. A few of these individuals were exceptional curlers. The leads and seconds on the Ken Watson Brier championship rinks were outstanding. Watson had Charlie Kerr and Marvin MacIntyre, respectively, on his team in 1936, Jim Grant and Charlie Scrymgeour in 1942, and Charlie Read and Lyle Dyker in 1949. Almost invariably these men out-curled the leads and seconds from opposing teams. Ken and Grant Watson recruited strong front ends for their teams. In fact, they did so a little too aggressively and blatantly to suit some people. They actually replaced players during an era when it was still the norm to change personnel only because of retirements or through mutual agreements.[54]

The McKnight brothers, E.R. ("Tommie") and Bill, played lead and second, respectively, for Ab Gowanlock's Glenboro rinks. They were strong sweepers and consistent shot-makers. In 1946, after Bill McKnight had moved to Winnipeg, he was the lead on Leo Johnson's Consols-winning team.[55]

Some other leads and seconds were also unusually skilled. Howard Wood's brother, Victor, was the second on the 1930 Brier-winning team, as well as the third on the 1925 British Consols champion team which did not compete for a Brier. Another Wood brother, Lionel, was the lead on both these teams and also on the 1945 British Consols winning team that did not get a chance to play in a Brier because of the war. Howard Wood's son, Howie Jr., was the young second on the 1940 Brier-winning team, who later skipped both grand aggregate and British Consols winners. Ray Stewart, who was with R.J. Gourley's Canadian champion team in 1931, may well have been the finest lead of his time. Marno Frederickson was Leo Johnson's lead on the 1934 Brier championship rink; later he became a top skip himself. Andy McWilliams was on

Three Winnipeg superstars showing their form: top left, Howard Wood, bottom left, Bill Walsh, and top right, Ken Watson. Bottom right, Ken Watson and friend demonstrating proper sweeping technique.

both the Bill Walsh Brier-winning teams. Bill Grant was the lead on both the 1928 and 1929 Gordon Hudson Brier champion teams. He was also part of the strongest teams Hudson ever had, the 1922 and 1923 grand-aggregate team of Bill Grant, Cliff Hudson, Alex Fiddler and Gordon Hudson.[56]

Jock Reid was the second and Harry Monk the lead on Jimmy Welsh's teams throughout Welsh's career as a top curler. They were not impressive draw-weight players, but they could hit consistently, and this was more important to Welsh because he preferred a hitting style. As Reid and Monk became older it was mentioned on occasion to Welsh that perhaps his front end should be changed. Welsh rejected this notion with a telling reply. No rink could have compiled the record his had over the years, he said, unless it possessed a competent front end. Besides, Reid and Monk were his "friends," and "harmony" among members of a team counted for a great deal.[57]

Harmony among the members of a team. What was Welsh talking about? He was referring to the ability of four individuals to get along with each other both on and off the ice. He was suggesting that good curling teams must be made up of people who appreciate each other's strengths and tolerate each other's weaknesses not only as curlers but as human beings.

Having brothers on the same team seemed conducive to this harmony. The Hudson, Wood, Watson and Welsh brothers curled together on top Winnipeg teams, and the McKnight brothers were part of the best rural Manitoba rink of the 1930s. The point can be documented further by adding that Leo Johnson's brother, Linc, was not a great shot-maker but he played on the front end of most of the strong Johnson teams; that in the 1920s and 1930s Ness Wise skipped one of the best teams in Winnipeg and had his brother, Cliff, playing with him for several years; and that the Garnet Campbell and Ernie Richardson rinks from Saskatchewan are only two of the many excellent teams from across the country that over the years have contained two or more brothers.

Why do brothers often curl with each other successfully? To answer this question, one can begin by observing that a curling team is a small unit. It contains only four people, not ten or twenty or more as do soccer, baseball, hockey or football teams. Moreover, at the highest levels of play, curling games are not decided by sheer skill so much as they are by the ability to concentrate and to make shots in pressure situations. More than athletes in most team sports, curlers need to know that their teammates care about them. They need people around them who genuinely want them to succeed but who will not desert them if they fail. Perhaps Jimmy Welsh articulated a more profound truth than he knew: a curler wants teammates who are true friends. Frequently it happens that your friend and your brother are the same person.[58]

Because they were composed of skilled players at every position who were able to cope with the psychological and interpersonal demands of competitive curling, from 1927 through 1957 Manitoba representatives, almost always from Winnipeg, won more than half the Brier championships. When they didn't win, normally they came close to doing so. Only once did a Manitoba team at the Canadian championship event lose more games than it won. This was in 1954 at Edmonton, when the Jimmy Welsh rink won four and lost six. The result in this particular year was disappointing. However, it was not surprising. The curlers across the country were becoming better and better, Brier observers noted.[59] The days were gone, it turned out, when curlers from Manitoba or any other province could dominate the event over several decades.

Between 1927 and 1957, Winnipeg's reputation as "the curling capital of

Canada"[60] rested on more than the exceptional record of the leading curlers. It also depended upon the health of the MCA and the continuing success of the annual bonspiel which it sponsored.

The MCA went through a few difficult years in the early to mid-1930s. In 1928 there were 126 clubs and 5,563 members in the association. In 1935–36 there were 124 clubs with only 4,386 members, and a few clubs in the southwestern, drought-stricken parts of the province survived only because their MCA dues were waived. In the late 1930s, however, the number of clubs and members began to increase again, and they did so all through the Second World War as well. Then, during the fifteen years after 1945, a curling boom occurred, and the number of clubs and members rose dramatically in Manitoba as they did across the country. Some of the figures from different years for the keystone province may be cited to observe the trends outlined above: 145 clubs and 4,973 members in 1938–39; 163 clubs and 5,178 members in 1943–44; 252 clubs and 11,594 members in 1948–49; 319 clubs and 15,984 members in 1954–55; 316 clubs and 17,152 members in 1959–60.[61]

In the period between 1927 and 1957, as in the previous one, the new clubs in the MCA were usually located in the agricultural service centres of the eastern prairies. However, they were now also frequently found in northern and eastern parts of Manitoba, where the fur trade was being replaced or complemented by commercial fishing, mining and electric-power development. In the 1930s, clubs were established in Flin Flon and Bissett, for example. In the 1940s and 1950s, others were founded in Moosehorn, Seven Sisters, Cranberry Portage and Lynn Lake.[62]

New clubs were also founded in Winnipeg, as well as in the surrounding suburbs, which were becoming more closely tied to the city proper. In 1929 the Assiniboine Memorial Club was formed in Assiniboia, west of St. James. In 1933 the Maple Leaf Club was established. In the same year the new St. Vital Club was formed; an earlier St. Vital Club had been formed in 1913 but had had only a brief existence. The Transcona Curling Club was established in 1938, although an earlier club in that railway suburb had existed from 1913 to 1919. After the Second World War, the Charleswood, Pembina, and Valour Road Legion clubs were founded in rapid succession, in 1946, 1947 and 1948 respectively; the Valour Road Legion Club soon became simply the Valour Road Club. The Winnipeg Winter Club, formed in 1929, introduced curling in 1951. Finally, two military curling clubs were founded, RCAF Station Winnipeg in 1956, and Army Fort Osborne in 1957. Meanwhile, four clubs had folded or become inactive. These were the Agricultural College, Telephones, St. John's, and University clubs. Two other clubs, the Civic and the Caledonian, amalgamated in 1938.[63]

The number of members in Winnipeg clubs cannot be documented as precisely or as often as the number in the province overall. In 1937 the number of members in city clubs was estimated at 1,400.[64] If this figure was accurate, membership had stabilized or even declined since the beginning of the Great Depression. By the mid-1940s there were about 3,200 members of Winnipeg clubs. However, at that time every club in the city was filled to the limit. Renters found it difficult to obtain ice, and for competitive curlers a negative consequence of the increased demand for curling time was the demise of the Tucker City Championship event which always had been played on ice made available without charge by city clubs.[65] No figures on membership are available for the late 1950s, but in the mid-1960s there were between 5,000 and 6,000 members in Winnipeg curling clubs.[66]

Between the mid-1920s and the mid-1950s, but particularly after the Second World War, certain ethnic groups in Manitoba began to take up curling for the first time in significant numbers. Before the 1920s, curlers usually were of Scottish, English or Irish descent, although in Winnipeg a few French-Canadian, Icelandic and Belgian names appeared on club rosters. By the late 1950s, more people from these latter groups had taken up the game, and so had many of the Germans, Ukrainians, Poles, Jews and other Europeans who had moved to Winnipeg and Manitoba by the tens of thousands between the late 1890s and the late 1920s.[67] In rural Manitoba by 1958, curling clubs had been founded in French-Canadian communities such as Letellier, Ste. Anne, St. Jean, St. Lazare and St. Pierre Jolys. Others had been formed in St. Claude, Ste. Rose du Lac, Mariapolis and Notre Dame de Lourdes, where the French-speaking people tended to be of Swiss, Belgian or European French descent. The first clubs had appeared also in Mennonite centres such as Altona, Steinbach and Rosenfeld, as well as in Ukrainian or Ukrainian-Polish communities such as Ethelbert and Sandy Lake. In the Interlake region, where a large percentage of the population had been of Icelandic descent since the 1870s, but where those of Ukrainian and Polish background had been growing more prominent since early in the new century, clubs were established in Teulon, Arborg, Ashern, Lundar, Eriksdale, Riverton and Gimli.[68] Meanwhile in Winnipeg, one club, the Maple Leaf, had been formed by, and largely for, Jewish people.[69] Other clubs had been joined by a fair number of individuals from non-British ethnic backgrounds. The Elmwood Curling Club has kept comparatively extensive membership records. The names of members suggest, if they do not prove, that curling developed wider appeal among non-British people. This club had one or more members named Felstead, Powlowich and Stucyk in the mid-1930s, one or more named Gretsinger, Ehn, Hauser, Kalansky and Laufersweiler in the early 1950s; in 1923–24 only one non-British name had appeared on the club roster – Schmidt. Moreover, by the 1950s, members of the executive bodies of Winnipeg clubs had names such as Kaminsky, Fenske and Demetrioff as well as Ferguson, Allan and Matthewson.[70]

The British-Protestant majority had always been confident that newcomers would be assimilated into Anglo-Canadian ways through curling and other sports. It seems likely that curling did contribute in some degree to the assimilation process, especially when only a few members of a minority group were part of a large club. But the roarin' game could be used also to retain a minority group identity. This is no doubt what the officers of the Canadian Ukrainian Athletic Club or the Belgian Club had in mind when they rented ice for their members. It is certainly what the people who established the Maple Leaf Curling Club wanted to do, and they probably succeeded in doing it. In their club, the Jewish people played or watched the same game that British or Belgian or Icelandic people did, but while doing so they talked about Jewish issues or characters. In 1949 the Maple Leaf Club even began to solidify a sense of community among western-Canadian Jews. In that year the club established the annual B'nai B'rith Bonspiel, which featured social occasions where Jewish friends and acquaintances from across the prairies could enjoy traditional food and drinks, and could share information and stories and laughter.[71]

Around the province and especially in Winnipeg, the average age of club members declined between the 1920s and the 1950s. No precise data on this is available, but after the Second World War several curlers noted that in their time participants in the sport had become younger and younger. To some degree this development resulted from the promotion of curling among young people by the MCA. About 1918, one Winnipeg club, the St. John's, facilitated a school curling club organized for students at St. John's Tech High School. Other clubs soon began to provide ice periodically for other schools, and in 1922 the first Winnipeg High School Bonspiel occurred. In 1927 the MCA established a committee to put on a bonspiel for Manitoba's young men up to twenty-one years of age. Then, in 1940, the association along with provincial authorities in physical education established the Provincial High School Bonspiel in Winnipeg during Christmas week. It quickly became the largest schoolboy bonspiel in the world. By 1947 there were 185 rinks taking part, and by 1955 there were 230 rinks. Meanwhile, in other provinces the MCA's idea caught on, and in 1950 nine provinces sent rinks to the first national schoolboy championship event.[72]

As it had in earlier periods, the MCA benefitted from the administrative skills and dedication of many officers. Among the presidents, Robert Jacob stands out. Jacob was one of the several MCA presidents who was prominent in the economic, political and cultural life of Winnipeg, of Manitoba and even of Canada. He was a lawyer and at different times a member of the Winnipeg School Board, attorney-general of the province, president of the Manitoba Lawn Bowling Association, and president of the Canadian Golf Association. At the annual meeting of the MCA held in April 1937, he was chosen president even though he had served in that office in 1926–27. The delegates to the meeting wanted the most capable man available to head the organization while it hosted another group of Scots curlers and sponsored its fiftieth anniversary bonspiel.[73]

The most dedicated officers of the MCA over extended periods of time were its unpaid secretaries, who followed J.P.

Robertson in the position. When Robertson resigned in 1918, J. Fred Palmer, a curling fanatic, father of Howard Palmer and one of the founders of the St. John's Club, became secretary for five years. He was succeeded by C.N. Harris, who filled the position from 1923 until illness and business pressures forced him to retire in 1937. The respect that members of the MCA, especially George J. Cameron, had for Charlie Harris is indicated by the fact that after his death the MacDonald Tobacco Company named the bonspiel's Grand Aggregate Trophy after him; in 1986 this trophy was re-named the Labatt Grand Aggregate Award. Gordon Hudson succeeded Harris on a temporary basis. It seemed he was always filling in for someone on short notice, and it's appropriate to note that Robert Jacob insisted that Hudson be his first vice-president during Jacob's second term as president. In 1939 Hudson was replaced by Steve Trewhitt. Besides running the bonspiel and the day-to-day affairs of the organization, Trewhitt promoted and oversaw annual club bonspiels instituted during the Second World War to raise money for the Red Cross. MCA members were justifiably proud of forwarding nearly $140,000 to the Red Cross between 1939 and 1945. Trewhitt resigned as secretary to become president in 1946. Bob O'Dowda of the Elmwood Curling Club succeeded him in the former position. He was the MCA's last unpaid secretary. When he resigned in 1952 to become first vice-president and then president, the decision was made to hire Vic Siddall as a full-time secretary with an honorarium.[74]

The main responsibilities of all the secretaries and of other MCA officers were to arrange for the annual bonspiel and to keep it running smoothly. The bonspiel was affected negatively by the economic pinch during the years of the Great Depression. In 1928 there were 188 rinks entered in the men's events, but for the next four years there were twenty, thirty and even forty rinks fewer. The finance committee found that they had difficulty raising the $8,000 or $9,000 required to run the event. This was the case especially after 1933 when the City of Winnipeg stopped making its annual donation, which by this time had reached $2,000 or $2,500. In 1934 the MCA started to charge non-curlers a small admission fee to watch the draws, and the 1936 decision to move the final two or three days of play to the Amphitheatre was made partly because more revenue could be generated there from spectators. A final new means of raising money was inaugurated in 1938: each visiting team began to pay an entry fee, although it was a smaller levy than the one that applied to city rinks.[75]

At the time bonspiel organizers were seeking ways to maintain revenues, they were also looking for means of cutting down on expenses. Beginning in 1933, big banquets were sacrificed, except on special occasions such as the fiftieth-anniversary bonspiel in 1938. Instead, in the 1930s, each visiting rink was taken out to a Winnipeg restaurant for one meal during their stay in the city, and then in the 1940s and 1950s receptions with a smorgasbord and perhaps entertainment were held either in a hotel or in the new Civic Auditorium on Vaughan Street. In 1938 another measure was introduced, partly to cut long-term costs and partly to make it easier to schedule games for the large number of rinks expected for the fiftieth-anniversary bonspiel. Winnipeg clubs were offered financial assistance to help them purchase matched sets of rocks for each sheet of ice. About $1,000 a year in annual cartage costs was eliminated in this way, and the curlers found the switch to club rather than individual stones more comfortable than they had expected.[76]

In the mid-1930s, the number of bonspiel entries begin to rise. There were only 158 rinks on hand in 1933, but 201 in 1934. By 1937 there were 240 and, except during the special year of 1938 when 346 teams showed up, the number of entries stayed at about 250 through 1943. Then the number of bonspiel teams increased dramatically, as did the number of MCA clubs and members. In 1944, 339 rinks entered. Exactly 400 did so in 1947, and in 1948, for the sixtieth-anniversary bonspiel, a record 454 entries participated. Thereafter the entries fell to a low of 330 in 1952, and in that particular year the Saskatchewan Curling Association's Bonspiel in Regina was bigger than the one in Winnipeg. But then the MCA's event drew larger numbers again until there were over 400 entries in 1958 and over 450 in 1959. It was, in the late 1950s, as it nearly always had been for seventy-five years, the world's biggest annual curling event.[77]

The number of teams that entered the veteran's event stayed at around two dozen, but the trends in the number of entries for the women's events were similar to those for regular men's competitions: in 1926 there were forty-one women's rinks; in 1930 there were sixty-seven; in 1936, eighty; in 1940, ninety-six; in 1947, 124; and in 1954, 110. The women's bonspiel was sponsored by the MLCA, but the draws were administered by MCA officials. They arranged for the women's competitions to begin a few days, or even a week, after the men's events were held, when two or three curling club buildings became available.

Between the 1920s and the 1960s the shot-making of the Winnipeg women's teams was not strong and did not enhance the city's reputation as a curling capital. In fact, for most bonspiels someone like Sadie Delmage of Dauphin or Lillie Clark of Portage la Prairie could put together a quartet that was better than those formed in Winnipeg. However, in these years women's curling was very much a recreational or social sport. Women were encouraged, even by other women, to obtain good, wholesome exercise through curling, but not to strive for excellence or victories. It was in hosting the largest women's bonspiel in the world, and in arranging social occasions such as the banquet held usually at the Fort Garry Hotel to inaugurate their bonspiel, that the Winnipeg women curlers added to Winnipeg's renown. They helped create the impression that Winnipeg was "wholly given over to curling for a fortnight," as Rev. Kerr had said in 1903.[78]

Sometimes it seemed that a fortnight wasn't long enough to complete the men's events. A one-week bonspiel was the goal of every secretary and executive committee. They never managed to attain it. Mild weather sometimes frustrated them, but their biggest problem was that the growth of curling facilities in Winnipeg did not keep pace with the increasing number of teams that wanted to play in the bonspiel.

There were new or improved facilities over the years, of course. Among the older clubs the West Kildonan in the 1930s, the Grain Exchange in the 1940s, and the Heather and Deer Lodge between 1956 and 1958, all moved to new locations or constructed new buildings at old sites. In doing so, however, they increased their total sheets of ice by only five. Two other older clubs, the CPR and the Eaton, arranged for the first time for their own buildings, but they simply acquired and fixed up existing structures: the CPR, which was renamed the Victoria Club in 1950, took over the Caledonian Club's facility on William Avenue, and the Eaton occupied the Grain Exchange's old rink, the one built at 111 Mayfair Avenue by the old Assiniboine Club. When it was formed in 1938, the Civic-Caledonian Club built a nice six-sheet rink on Sherbrook Street, but the new sheets only balanced those that were lost a couple of years earlier when the Civic had abandoned its facility on Pacific Avenue. As for the new clubs, the Maple Leaf simply rented ice for more than a dozen years before acquiring the St. John's Club rink when that club folded in 1946. The St. Vital

Club, formed in 1933, waited until 1937 before building a four-sheet facility at St. Anne's Road and Fermor. In the early 1950s this rink became a six-sheeter, and then in 1956 the club moved to a building with the same number of sheets at St. Anne's and Regal. As soon as they were founded, the Charleswood, Pembina, and Valour Road clubs built new rinks on Grant Avenue, Pembina Highway, and Burnell streets, respectively. By late in the 1950s, these three facilities contained a total of fourteen sheets of ice. When it added curling, the Winnipeg Winter Club incorporated four sheets of ice into its existing building at River and Donald. Once established in the mid-1950s, the two military clubs, the Fort Osborne and the RCAF, used buildings containing a total of seven sheets. The effect of all of these changes, along with the disappearance of rinks once available through the Telephone and University clubs, meant that in 1959 bonspiel organizers had 102 sheets of regular curling ice for 458 rinks. For the 1944 bonspiel the organizers had only seventy-six sheets for 339 rinks. Back in 1928 they had had sixty-five sheets for 188 teams, a much better ratio. Of course in 1944 and 1959, organizers could have utilized the facilities of the Assiniboine Memorial and Transcona clubs, but evidently they felt these were located too far from the centre of the city.[79]

In these circumstances, in order to make sure the bonspiel did not last longer than two weeks, the organizers went beyond their previous restrictions on the number of "open" events in which a rink could win prizes, and limited the open events in which a specific team could be "alive" at any given time. By 1954 a simple "two-string" draw had been inaugurated for open events. There were five events on each of two sides, and a rink went "down a string" as it was knocked out of events on each side. Once it lost ten games in total, a team was out of the bonspiel. MCA officials also reduced the

Robert Jacob

J. Fred Palmer

Women's curling team, 1946

R.D. Waugh

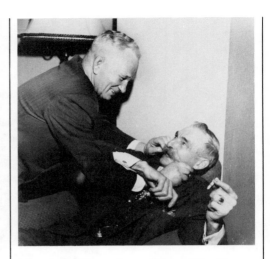

Two popular members of the curling frater-nity, Alex Stewart and George "Handle-bars" Henderson, sharing a laugh.

Four legends in conversation. L to R: Gor-don Hudson, Ken Watson, Bill Walsh and Ab Gowanlock, 1952.

Ab "Spats" Gowanlock, his famous spats being adjusted by a friend

Howard "Pappy" Wood and Bill Walsh sharing a coffee, 1957

Jim Ursel (left) and Norm Houck (second from right) playing cribbage with two friends in the Strathcona Curling Club

number of "closed" events. These events had been prominent since 1891. Teams had to qualify for them, usually through district playoffs or by being selected by their clubs or an MCA committee. Naturally, teams that gained the right to compete in the closed events tended to be the teams that did well in the open ones, and frequently one event had to be delayed while games in another were completed. That the reduction in closed events had a positive effect is illustrated by the result in 1950, when a Bill McTavish rink from the Elmwood Curling Club became the first to go through the bonspiel undefeated. They played only twenty-two games rather than the thirty-five or forty they would have had to play (if they had kept winning) under previous formats. By 1954 there was only one closed event, the one for veterans, whereas in 1926 there had been four other closed events as well.[80]

An outstanding feature of the bonspiels held from the mid-1930s through the late 1940s was the high percentage of non-Winnipeg clubs that entered. From 1929 through 1933, visiting teams were not as prominent as they had been earlier. Usually they did not make up half the total number of teams on hand. However, from 1934 through 1949, the number of visiting rinks always exceeded the number of city ones, usually by a good margin. In fact, from 1943 through 1946 there were more than twice as many visiting rinks as city ones entered.[81]

This development was stimulated by several factors. In the 1930s, members of city clubs began to make goodwill tours by train to play against members of rural clubs, and rural curlers occasionally returned the visits.[82] The effort to raise money for the Red Cross during the Second World War, led by the friendly but determined Steve Trewhitt, gave rural and urban clubs a stronger sense of common purpose than they had ever had before.[83] But the rural curlers had essentially the same reasons for

coming to the Winnipeg Bonspiel as they always had. They wanted good fellowship and keen competition.

Most of them wanted to get together with old friends or make new ones. They did so at the annual reception, or before the curlers' church service. Perhaps also they met in the locker, or "snake," room in the basement of a Winnipeg curling club and passed a bottle of liquor around illegally. Perhaps they gathered in a bar at a hotel, which probably had been granted the right to stay open for extended hours. Perhaps they met in a curler's private room at the hotel; from 1924 to 1938, R.D. Waugh, a former mayor of Winnipeg and a past-president of the MCA, was a useful man to know if the curlers wanted to keep a party going long into the night, because during these years he was the chairman of the Manitoba Liquor Commission.[84] The curlers might talk about business. They might exchange jokes. They would reminisce about great, or at least intriguing, curling shots they had witnessed over the years. Frequently they spoke in awe of the beautiful delivery of a Dunbar in the past or a Watson in the present. On the other hand they also laughed as they recalled someone's awkward sweeping style, or as they spoke of someone losing his balance as he came out of the hack, missing the broom by half the width of a sheet of ice. Human beings almost always laugh when they see a body which acts independently of the mind that should be in control of it.[85] Curlers were drawn to their sport partly because they could witness and then talk about comical events that occurred on the ice.

The rural curlers wanted to do more than socialize; they also wanted a crack at the top Winnipeg teams. Too frequently it happened that one of them knocked off a Welsh or a Johnson or a Wood, then celebrated so enthusiastically that they could not recover to beat anyone else. The better rural teams, led by such people as Gowanlock of Glenboro, Pritchard of Killarney, A.H. Hume of Oak River, J.W. Hewitt of Melita, W.L. Adams of Newdale or Gordon Taylor of Rivers, knew that the bonspiel was to a significant degree a test of consistency and endurance, and that one well-played game was not of much consequence.[86]

The rural teams skipped by these men as well as by some others came to the bonspiel with victories as much as alcohol in mind. They especially wanted to represent Manitoba in the Brier. Until 1949, except for a short time in the early 1930s when the grand-aggregate winner automatically went to Toronto, the Manitoba representative was the winner of a special event which opened during the second week of the bonspiel. Normally, in order to qualify for this event, one had to reach a certain point in an open event, say "the eights" or "the sixteens." In any case, you had to enter the MCA's Winnipeg Bonspiel in order to represent the keystone province in the Canadian championship event.[87]

Over the years, rural Manitoba curlers complained frequently if not bitterly about this arrangement. They contended that too many good curlers could not leave their jobs or farms or families to spend two weeks in Winnipeg. After the Second World War the MCA appointed a committee to look into the matter and suggest a course of action. In 1948, the members of the committee recommended that a system of zones be set up so that district winners, as well as rinks reaching given points in the bonspiel's open events, would qualify for the Consols playdowns. The MCA accepted the recommendation. The playdowns would still be held in Winnipeg after the bonspiel, but beginning in 1949, teams did not have to go through the bonspiel in order to win the Consols Trophy.[88]

There can be no doubt that the new way of selecting a provincial representative was fairer than the old to every curler in Manitoba. There can be no doubt as well that it had an immense effect on the bonspiel. In the short run it helped cause the bonspiel to become less important to rural curlers that it had been. In 1949, 224 of 406 teams in the bonspiel were visiting ones, but the year before, 272 of 454 had been. In 1950 there were 175 visiting rinks among the total of 364 that entered; in 1951 there were 145 of 348; in 1952 there were 137 of 330; in 1953 there were 157 of 374. Through the rest of the 1950s, rural rinks never came close to making up half the total.[89] The change in the Consols format was not the most important reason the bonspiel became a city event to a greater extent than it had been, but it was certainly one of them.

The new format also helped cause the bonspiel to become less a competitive and more a social curling experience. The grand-aggregate winner was no longer the unofficial world, or even provincial, champion in the sport. Most of the best curlers in the province still showed up, of course, and normally they won the most prestigious events. But many of them entered the bonspiel with a Consols spot already won through zone play. They did not curl with the sense of finality that great athletes have when at the top of their game. They might be working on certain strategies or types of shots, or they may be having fun before the serious shot-making got under way a week or two later.

In the late 1950s, then, the MCA Bonspiel was still the greatest bonspiel in the world and it was still a main reason Winnipeg was a renowned curling city.[90] It was becoming prominent for different reasons, however, from ones that had existed thirty years earlier. It had begun to change dramatically. So had the curling world of which it was a part. In the three decades after the late 1950s, the changes in the bonspiel and in curling became significantly more pronounced and more discernible.

4

Still a Special Place,
1957 to 1988

From late in the 1950s to late in the 1980s, Manitobans and Winnipeggers did not dominate competitive curling as they had in earlier decades. However, Winnipeg remained a special place in the curling world. One reason was that the city produced such a large number of top curlers, and the ones who represented their province and country compiled an enviable record. A second reason was that so many curlers from across Canada and around the world had learned, or were learning, from Winnipeggers how to curl competitively. A third was the relationship between the members of the Winnipeg media and curling, especially the extensive coverage the various outlets gave the sport and the ways in which Winnipeg television producers and technicians pioneered means for broadcasting it. A fourth factor was that so many successful national and international championship events were held there. They were arranged by officers of the MCA and the MLCA which were, respectively, among the largest men's and women's curling organizations in the country. Finally, Winnipeg was still the site of the biggest annual bonspiel in the world.

BETWEEN THE 1950s and the 1980s an important development in Canadian and world curling was the establishment of a number of national and international championship events. A national men's championship had been created in 1927. A world championship was added in 1959, although until 1968 it was not officially recognized as such because a world curling organization was formed only in 1966. A national high-school boys'championship had been held for the first time in 1950. This event evolved in the 1970s into a national junior men's championship (with an age limit of nineteen in 1988); in 1975 a world junior men's championship was founded. A Canadian women's championship tournament was established in 1961, and a world championship tournament followed in 1979. A national junior women's event was first held in 1972, and a world junior event in 1988. Other Canadian championship events were first created for mixed rinks in 1964, for senior men's rinks in 1965, and for senior

Ken Watson (left) receiving the Elmer Freytag Award for contributions to the development of international curling

Ina Light

Canadian women's champions, 1965. L to R: Peggy Casselman, skip; Val Taylor, third; Pat McDonald, second; Pat Scott, lead.

Enthusiastic crowd welcomes home the Casselman rink, Canadian champions, 1965

women's teams in 1973 (in 1988 a curler became a senior at the age of fifty). Of course the founding of these national and international championships was preceded or accompanied by the creation of provincial championship events in the different categories of curling.[1]

The Canadian and world championship events were either founded by or eventually recognized by one of three national or international curling organizations. The first was the Dominion Curling Association (DCA), which was formed in 1935 and which became the Canadian Curling Association (CCA) in 1968. The second was the Canadian Ladies' Curling Association (CLCA), which was established in 1961. The third was the International Curling Federation (ICF), which was founded in 1966. Although Winnipegger John T. Haig was chosen the first president of the DCA, there is no reason to believe that Winnipeggers or Manitobans were more influential than others in founding the three organizations. They were, however, important in establishing some of the championship events.

Ken Watson was the man primarily responsible for setting up a national high-school championship. In the 1940s he had worked to inaugurate the provincial high-school bonspiel held annually in Winnipeg during the week between Christmas and New Year's Day. He also had arranged with representatives of the *Winnipeg Free Press*, the *Regina Leader-Post*, the *Saskatoon Star-Phoenix*, and Taylor-Pearson-Carson, an automotive parts wholesale firm that operated out of British Columbia and Alberta, to establish first a Saskatchewan-Manitoba and then a western Canadian championship in the late 1940s. In 1950 the western Canadian championship had become a national one, sanctioned and to some extent financed by the DCA.

Watson had not accomplished all of this by himself, of course. He had had a lot of help, especially from fellow Winnipeggers

such as teammates C.H. "Charlie" Scrymgeour and Lyle Dyker, MCA administrator Bill Lumsden, and *Free Press* sportswriter Maurice Smith. But in the 1940s and early 1950s Watson had been the man with the energy and influence to keep building a bigger, more prestigious championship event. He was also the man who, in 1958, arranged with Frank McIntosh, president of the Pepsi-Cola Company in Canada and a former Winnipegger who had once curled out of Ken Watson's first club, the St. John's, to have Pepsi sponsor the Canadian high-school boys' championship. In 1988 Pepsi sponsored the Canadian junior men's event for the thirty-first consecutive year, as well as the Canadian junior women's for the eighth.[2]

Watson was also the key Canadian in the genesis of the Scotch Cup series of matches, which evolved into the world men's curling championship and which from 1968 through 1985 was known as the Air Canada Silver Broom. The idea of an annual competition between the champion rinks of Scotland and Canada really originated with two Scotsmen: Robin Welsh, secretary of the RCCC, and Jock Waugh, member of the Scotch Whisky Association. Once Waugh's association had agreed in principle to sponsor such a competition and to provide a trophy for the winner, a representative of Houston Agencies, a Toronto public relations firm acting on behalf of the Scotch Whisky Association, invited Watson to travel to Scotland to meet with advocates of the Scotland-vs.-Canada championship. Watson flew across the Atlantic early in 1959, and out of the meetings he attended came arrangements for a five-game series between Scottish and Canadian champions to be known as the Scotch Cup.

Watson's actions were bold. He went to Scotland without the approval of the DCA, though he informed certain individual officers of the Association of his plans. But Watson was confident that Canada's competitive curlers would respond positively to an opportunity to travel to Scotland at the expense of the Scotch Whisky Association. His confidence was justified. Before the Brier was completed early in March of that year, the teams from every province had indicated that if they won the Canadian championship they would play in the Scotch Cup. The Ernie Richardson rink from Saskatchewan earned the chance to make the trip overseas, and they took it.

For helping to arrange the initial Scotch Cup series, Watson was subjected to a good deal of criticism from officials of the DCA. These officials objected among other things to Canadian curlers becoming closely associated with, and to some degree beholden to, a whisky company. Mostly the officials resented Watson's failure to work through the DCA. In his defence, Watson said that speedy and secret negotiations were necessary if arrangements were to be concluded in time for matches to be held at the end of the curling season of 1958-59. The DCA withheld sanction of the first Scotch Cup series. The games proceeded anyway. The next year the DCA recognized the event, partly because representatives of the Scotch Whisky Association and of Scottish curling apologized for not having used proper channels. Meanwhile the DCA had both rewarded and punished Watson by making him an honorary life member. This decision recognized his outstanding curling career, but also made him ineligible for high office in the association.[3]

Winnipeggers also played key roles in establishing the national senior, world junior, world women's, and world junior women's championship events. Bill Lumsden was a vice-president of the DCA in the mid-1960s and the man most responsible for negotiating with Seagram Distilleries to sponsor the first Canadian senior men's championship in 1964. Bob Picken served as delegate from the CCA to the ICF from 1973 to 1981. He did so with such

energy and skill that in 1987 the ICF made him the second Winnipegger to win the prestigious Elmer Freytag award for outstanding contributions to international curling; Ken Watson was the first. Picken worked with delegates from other countries to create the world junior men's and the world women's championships; he and his associates had to convince other members of the ICF and the whole curling community that interest in the world men's championship would not decline if new world championships were inaugurated. Finally, Ina Light, the Winnipegger who served as CLCA delegate to the ICF from 1985 to 1988, was the curling official most responsible for creating the world junior women's championship.[4]

In the three decades from 1958 to 1988 Manitobans performed admirably in the new, larger world of competitive curling they had helped to create. They won thirty-two national and five world titles. Yet, in most years curling enthusiasts in the province were disappointed in the record of Manitoba's teams. They seemed to feel that in every season their teams should be as successful or almost as successful as they had been in 1964–65 and 1983–84. In the former year Manitoba rinks won three of the five national titles available. In the latter they won five of the seven national championships and one of the three world championships. Like most Canadians, Manitobans were bewildered by the success the Europeans had in world championships. Manitobans also were surprised by the number of national events won by British Columbians and Ontarians: from 1958 through 1988 they won twenty-four and fourteen, respectively. The most important and most disconcerting facts of all to Manitobans were that Saskatchewan and Alberta won more national and world titles than they themselves did. Saskatchewan took thirty-nine national and six world championships from 1958 through 1988.

Canadian women's champions, 1967. L to R: Dot Rose, lead; Laurie Bradawaski, second; Joan Ingram, third; Betty Duguid, skip.

Canadian women's champions, 1978. L to R: Cathy Pidzarko, skip; Chris Pidzarko, third; Iris Armstrong, second; Patti Vande, lead.

*Canadian and world women's champions,
1984. Clockwise from left: Corinne Peters,
second; Janet Arnott, lead; Chris More
(nee Pidzarko), third; Connie Laliberte,
skip.*

Cathy and Chris Pidzarko, Canadian junior women's champions in 1972 and 1974. One of several sets of twins who have won championships in women's curling. Others are the Laliberte, Fallis, Ellwood and Thomson twins.

Canadian senior men's champions, 1965. L to R: Cliff Wise, lead; Leo Johnson, skip; Marno Frederickson, third; Fred Smith, second.

Canadian senior men's champions, 1973. L to R: Harry Sulkers, lead; John McLean, second; Norm McLean, third; Bill McTavish, skip.

Lloyd Gunnlaugson, Canadian senior men's champion in 1982, 1983 and 1984

Canadian mixed champions, 1973. L to R: Susan Lynch, lead; Barry Fry, skip; Steve Decter, second; Peggy Casselman, third.

Canadian mixed champions of 1988, shown here in action in 1989 Canadian championships in Brandon. Skip Jeff Stoughton encouraging sweepers Rob Meakin, Lynn Morrow (hidden) and Karen Fallis.

Canadian junior men's champions, 1979.
Clockwise from top left: Mike Friesen,
lead; Joel Gagne, second; Lyle Derry,
third, Mert Thompsett, skip.

Brier winners, 1965. L to R: Ron Braun-
stein, second; Terry Braunstein, skip; Don
Duguid, third; Ray Turnbull, lead.

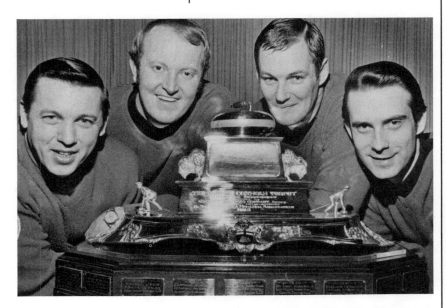

Brier and world championship winners, 1970 and 1971. L to R: Don Duguid, skip; Bryan Wood, lead; Jim Pettapiece, second; Rod Hunter, third.

Brier and world championship winners, 1972. L to R: Orest Meleschuk, skip; Dave Romano, third; John Hanesiak, second; Pat Hailley, lead.

Brier winners, 1979. L to R: Barry Fry, skip; Bill Carey, third; Gord Sparkes, second; Bryan Wood, lead.

Brier winners, 1981. L to R: Kerry Burtnyk, skip; Mark Olson, third; Jim Spencer, second; Ron Kammerlock, lead.

Brier winners, 1984. L to R: Mike Riley, skip; Brian Toews, third; John Helston, second; Russ Wookey, lead. On parade float at world championship in Duluth, 1984.

Over the same thirty-one years, Alberta captured thirty-six Canadian titles and seven world ones.[5] In the 1960s, 1970s and 1980s, Manitobans in general and Winnipeggers in particular had to admit that when people thought of excellence in curling their province and city did not come to mind as automatically as they had in earlier decades.

Since it was only in men's curling that a reorganized national championship event existed before the 1950s, it was only in men's curling that valid comparisons between pre- and post-1950s performances could be made. Furthermore, it was always accepted that the most skillful curling and the very best teams were found in the regular men's category, not in the women's, mixed or age-limit categories. In the men's category Manitobans compiled a fine record, but curlers from Alberta and Saskatchewan accumulated better ones, and those from Northern Ontario and Ontario produced surprisingly good ones. From 1958 through 1988, Manitoba teams won seven of thirty-one Canadian championships, and Manitoba representatives in the Brier won sixty-three percent of their games.[6] During the same years, Saskatchewan representatives took six Briers and sixty-seven percent of their Brier games, and Alberta's representatives won nine Briers and seventy-three percent of their games. Manitoba's Brier winners were all from Winnipeg, and three of them went on to capture the world championship. Both Alberta's and Saskatchewan's Brier winners won five world titles. Each of Ontario's and Northern Ontario's three Brier winners moved on to take two world titles.[7] The Winnipeg men certainly were competitive on the national and international scene, but not dominant.

Furthermore, from the late-1950s to the late-1980s, curling's superstars often came not from Winnipeg but from elsewhere. At almost any time from the mid-1920s through the mid-1950s, two or three of the top Winnipeg curlers – Hudson, Wood, Gourley, Congalton, Johnson, Watson, Welsh, Walsh – had been the biggest names in the sport. But in the late 1950s the biggest names were Garnet Campbell of Saskatchewan and Matt Baldwin of Alberta; in the early 1960s they were Ernie Richardson of Saskatchewan and Hec Gervais of Alberta; in the late 1960s they were Ron Northcott of Alberta and perhaps Bob Pickering of Saskatchewan; through most of the 1970s and 1980s they were one or more of Ed Lukowich and Pat Ryan of Alberta, Al Hackner of Northern Ontario, Bud Somerville of the United States, Eigil Ramsfjell of Norway.

The primary reason Winnipeg curlers were not consistently mentioned when the very best curlers were identified was that only three of the seven Winnipeg teams that won the Brier went on to win the world championship. Moreover, one of the skips who won the world title, Orest Meleschuk, did so through a kind of fluke. In 1972, on the last end of the final game against Bob LaBonte of the United States, Meleschuk was down nine to seven, with last-rock advantage. When he went to throw his final stone, Meleschuk had second shot, but LaBonte had the shot and third-shot rocks. Meleschuk's throw knocked LaBonte's shot rock out of the house, but Meleschuk's shooter evidently rolled further away from the button than LaBonte's other stone, which meant Meleschuk would count one and lose the match nine to eight. However, just as Meleschuk's shooter stopped, the USA third, Frank Aasand, threw his arms up and indicated victory; his skip, LaBonte, leapt in the air a moment later. But when LaBonte came down, he inadvertently kicked the stone Meleschuk had just thrown. At this point no one from Meleschuk's team had conceded victory to LaBonte, and probably the Canadians would have asked an umpire to measure, just in case it might show they had scored the deuce. But now one of the rocks had been moved. After a good deal of discussion, it was determined that the Canadians should be given two points. Meleschuk won the game in the extra end.[8]

The unusual circumstances of his 1972 victory, plus his whole curling record over the years, meant Meleschuk was recognized as a very fine curler, but not a star of the same magnitude as Richardson, Northcott and the others just mentioned. The only Winnipegger and Manitoban who shone as splendidly as these superstars was Don Duguid, the man who skipped Manitoba's two other world-championship winners.

Duguid was born and raised in Winnipeg, and started throwing curling rocks in the mid-1940s at the age of nine at the Victoria Curling Club, where his father was the ice maker. He became a serious curler as a teenager, partly because he could see that his small body always would in the future be a handicap in the body-contact sports he enjoyed and at which he was proficient. In 1953, at the age of seventeen, he began to curl with Howard Wood, Sr., on a Granite Club team. In 1956 he joined Howard Wood, Jr., and played second on "Howie's" third-place finisher at the Brier held in Kingston in 1957. He began to skip his own rink in 1962–63, and in that year his team won the grand aggregate at the MCA Bonspiel. In 1964 he became the third for Terry Braunstein, the man who had skipped the youngest team ever to appear in a Brier, the 1958 Manitoba rink that lost in a playoff to Matt Baldwin of Alberta. In 1965 Braunstein's team won the Canadian championship, and Duguid's superb shot-making at third was a major reason for the victory. Duguid then stayed with Braunstein through the 1968–69 season. In fact they won the grand aggregate at the 1969 MCA Bonspiel, although by this time the two men had switched positions on their team.

In the summer of 1969 Duguid decided he would sit out the next year, but in December he received a call from Rod Hunter that changed his plans. Hunter was part of a solid Winnipeg team that he and his brother, John, had formed a few years earlier; Rod and John Hunter had skipped and played second, respectively, Jim Pettapiece had played third, and Bryan Wood had been lead. John Hunter always had been a serious student, and when the 1969 MCA Bonspiel came along he decided not to compete. Clare Payne was his substitute, with Payne skipping the team and Rod Hunter and Pettapiece each "dropping down" one position. The same arrangement was made the next year, 1969–70, when John Hunter stopped curling competitively. For various reasons Payne didn't fit in with his new teammates, so Rod Hunter phoned Duguid to ask if Duguid would skip the team.

Duguid accepted the offer, and during the rest of the 1969–70 season and then during the 1970–71 season he, Hunter, Pettapiece and Wood formed the dominant team in curling. They won the grand aggregate at the MCA Bonspiel in 1970 and one of the major events in 1971. They won the Brier and the Silver Broom in both years. They lost a total of three games in the two Briers and went undefeated in the two Silver Broom championships. They split up after the 1970–71 season because Duguid had had his fill of competitive curling; Duguid says now, in a matter-of-fact fashion, that his team was good enough to win three or four more world championships.[9]

Duguid may have been the most accurate hitter in the history of curling. He used to near-perfection the "tuck" delivery. The tuck evolved more or less naturally out of the "Winnipeg" or "Watson" slide. This slide had been developed on leather-soled but rubber-heeled shoes; naturally the Watson brothers and other early long sliders placed weight on the ball of the front foot.

The tuck delivery represented essentially a slide with an exaggerated bend of the front knee and with the weight more on the toes than on the ball of the lead foot. The front foot was tucked under the body.

Young Winnipeg curlers of Duguid's generation were the first to utilize the tuck, and Winnipeggers have been identified with it ever since. Even though the evolution of curling shoes in the 1960s, 1970s and 1980s made it possible to use a long slide and keep the front foot reasonably flat on the ice, Winnipeggers such as Duguid, Barry Fry, Kerry Burtnyk and Jeff Stoughton, as well as people such as Pat Ryan of Alberta, who learned to curl in Winnipeg but made their reputation elsewhere, continued to use the tuck and to enjoy success while doing so. By the late 1980s, keen students of curling had identified the negative consequences of employing the tuck. They had found that there is a good chance that injury will occur to the front knee. Furthermore, a tucker tends to control weight through drive from the leg rather than through swing from the arm, and the big muscles in the leg cannot control the force they apply as precisely as the smaller muscles in the arm and shoulder can; this means the tucker normally does not have the pinpoint weight control that the flat-footed shooter can develop. On the other hand, students of the delivery recognize that tuckers can place their heads lower than flat-footed throwers can. The tucker is therefore in a better position to hit the broom perfectly. Duguid was probably more consistently accurate than anyone. Moreover, he had the short, thick legs that seem best able to withstand the wear and tear caused by the tuck; he preferred to hit rather than to draw; and he was confident his sweepers would make appropriate adjustments in his weight once the rock left his hand. In other words he had the type of body, the strategy, and even the personality that could use the tuck most effectively.[10]

Although Duguid was an exceptional shot-maker – there are well-informed people who say he was the greatest ever – Winnipeg and Manitoba no longer produced the majority of curling's superstars. Furthermore, from the late 1950s to the late 1980s, Manitoba and Winnipeg teams were not as successful in major championships as they once had been. Why didn't they do better?

Various answers to this question were offered in the 1960s, 1970s and 1980s. Three of these answers are closely related to each other.[11] First, sometimes a lack of harmony seemed a problem on the rink representing Manitoba; in 1957 and 1973, to give two examples, the members of the team in the Brier did not benefit from each other's friendship the way the members of Gordon Hudson's, Jimmy Welsh's or Leo Johnson's rinks once had. Second, teams no longer stayed together year in and year out, through good times and bad. If a team did not enjoy success within a year or two of formation, the members split up and often even joined new clubs in order to become part of a promising new rink. Third, especially in the 1960s, the front ends of Manitoba teams were weaker than those of top rinks from other provinces. Good leads and seconds seemed less content than they once had been to play the less prestigious positions. Perhaps more of them should have done as Bryan Wood did in the 1970s. He was the lead on the Duguid world championship teams of 1970 and 1971. When Duguid retired, Wood played lead for a year for Rod Hunter. Then he skipped his own team for a season, but he realized while doing so that he could not make the great shots a skip must make periodically. He also realized he possessed skills that were most useful at lead. In particular he could quickly and accurately judge the speed of a rock once it left a teammate's hand, and this made him a very effective sweeper. Wood went back to playing the lead position in

1973–74, and by the end of the 1978–79 season he had been part of one more national and three more provincial championship teams.[12]

Possibly a bigger reason than the three just mentioned for the lack of Manitoba success was that the province, and especially its capital city, "exported" so many top curlers. This was particularly true during the 1970s when Manitoba's economy did not boom the way the economy of other provinces did. For example, at the Brier in 1972 the skip of the Nova Scotia team was Barry Shearer, who had learned to curl at Winnipeg's Strathcona Club. At the same Brier the skip of the Quebec rink was Bill Kent of Virden, who previously had skipped Quebec's Brier representative in 1963 and 1970. In 1972 as well, Jim Ursel of Winnipeg moved to Montreal. He had been the third on Norm Houck's strong Strathcona Club Brier team in 1962. He stayed in Montreal until 1980, when he moved back to Winnipeg. In the eight years he spent in Quebec, Ursel took six teams to the Brier, and his team won the event in 1977. As part of their Quebec teams, Kent or Ursel sometimes had with them fellow Manitobans Art Lobel, Murray Gregga, Bill Ross and Alf Berting. Harvey Mazinke skipped the Saskatchewan team that won the Brier in 1973; he had learned to curl in the Strathcona Club's junior program and had thrown third stones on the fine Bruce Hudson rink from the Strathcona that represented Manitoba at the 1964 Brier. Finally, in 1979, when twelve of the forty-eight curlers in the Brier were Manitobans, all four members of the Paul Devlin Alberta team were former Winnipeggers. The second on that rink was Pat Ryan who, by 1989, had skipped four Alberta Brier representatives; two of his teams won Canadian championships and one captured a world title.[13]

The other prairie provinces also lost some good curlers, of course, and some-times they lost them to Manitoba. Dan Fink, for example, was the skip of the Manitoba team in the 1973 Brier. He was from Saskatchewan. So was his second, Jim Pettapiece, who had been second on both Don Duguid's world-championship teams.[14] But the great number of curlers from Winnipeg and Manitoba who represented other provinces in national and world events tended to support the impression, held by many curling observers, that the city and province produced more fine curlers than others, even if they didn't produce the majority of the superstars. Certainly this was something Larry Taylor felt in 1987. He had been a high-calibre curler in Manitoba before he moved to Alberta in 1984. He soon concluded that the Pat Ryan and Ed Lukowich teams from his new province might well be the best two teams in the world, but that there were only about six or seven "quality" rinks in Alberta. There were, he said, nearly that many in the Brandon district, and there were "twenty to thirty in Winnipeg."[15]

A number of reasons then, caused Manitoba's teams from the late 1950s to the late 1980s to be weaker than they might have been. But the biggest reason these teams did not win national and international championships repeatedly was that curlers from outside their city and province had become better than they had been. One indication of this is the number of ends that were blanked in Brier games. A blank end usually occurs when most of the first fifteen shots are made perfectly or near-perfectly, and the skip with last rock decides not to accept one point. In the 1958 Brier there were thirty blank ends. In 1961 there were fifty-two; in 1963 there were ninety-one. In 1974 there were 120 blank ends at the lowest-scoring Brier in history to that point.[16] By late in the 1980s blank ends were so common that it was possible a rule change soon would be made to remove the incentive for purposely failing to score. In

108

the 1960s, 1970s and 1980s, the best Winnipeg curlers regularly shot eighty percent, which means not that they missed one in five attempts, but only that they failed to make all their shots perfectly. Their problem was that too often the best curlers from across the country and around the world did as well as or better than they did.

A major reason curlers from many locations improved and caught up to the Winnipeggers was that curling became an artificial-ice sport in the 1940s, 1950s and 1960s. Playing surfaces became straighter and more predictable, and the advantages Winnipeggers once had gained from their superior natural-ice conditions disappeared. A second reason applied to curlers from the prairies in particular. They benefitted from the better roads and better automobiles available after the Second World War. These roads and autos could be used virtually all winter. Their presence meant that big bonspiels became viable at which thousands of dollars or new cars were the top prizes; at these events and at smaller bonspiels, better curlers from rural Manitoba, from Saskatchewan and from Alberta could now compete against each other regularly, just as better Winnipeg curlers always had.[17] Finally, among the many reasons curlers from Canada and all over the world became better at the sport was the instruction Winnipeggers had given or were giving them.

Some curlers across the Dominion had learned from Ken Watson's four books and his instructional columns, which for a time in the early 1950s appeared in some four-dozen Canadian newspapers. In 1979 Jack Matheson of the *Winnipeg Tribune* exaggerated when he said it was "all Ken's fault" that the world had become the equal of Manitoba in curling, but his remark contained a point worth making.[18] Meanwhile, in southern British Columbia several curlers had learned from the example and instruction provided by Mac Braden, Billy

Finlay and Frank Avery; in fact, Lyle Dagg of Vancouver, who skipped the Canadian and world-champion team in 1964, was a Finlay-Avery protege.[19] In what became the real hotbed of serious curling in the United States, the Hibbing-Eveleth-Duluth-Superior region of northeastern Minnesota and northwestern Wisconsin, a competitive approach to the sport had been popularized and promoted especially by Bob Dunbar in the 1910s, 1920s and 1930s, and by his son "Bobby" Dunbar in the 1940s and 1950s.[20] Finally, in Europe, the curlers who won seven world championships between 1973 and 1988 did so in large part because they had been exposed to the ideas and energy of a Winnipegger named Ray Turnbull.

Turnbull became interested in curling in the mid-1950s when he was a student at Kelvin High School. He took up the game, in truth, because he knew that by doing so he could meet and be around a girl who had caught his eye. Soon he started curling with Terry Braunstein, another student at Kelvin. A couple of years later, in 1958, they went to the Brier in Victoria. All the members of that Manitoba Brier team were under twenty-one and too young to drink legally. This meant that some of the normal rituals asssociated with the Brier had to be adjusted. For example, Gooderham and Worts, distillers, provided Braunstein's rink with a case of soft drinks rather than the customary case of whisky they gave the other teams. (It did not take long for curlers from other provinces to find out that the Manitobans had "free mix.") The DCA quickly passed a rule to make sure an underage team did not appear in the Brier again. Turnbull stayed with Braunstein after 1958 and was the lead on his 1965 Brier championship team. Turnbull still curls with Braunstein whenever he has a chance to do so.

In 1968 Turnbull and Don Duguid watched some of the games in the Canadian Ladies' Curling Championship held at the

Ray Turnbull demonstrating correct delivery at one of his curling clinics

St. James Civic Centre. They were appalled, but mostly amazed, at how poorly some of the better women curlers threw and swept rocks. Turnbull and Duguid knew that they could help these women through instruction in basic curling techniques, and decided to hold a clinic that fall. They invited Wally Ursuliak of Edmonton to assist them. Ursuliak had been on a Brier-winning Alberta team in 1961; more important, he sold curling equipment, and some of the students would likely want to purchase brooms, sweaters or footwear. Turnbull prepared some presentations on the fundamental skills of the sport, and Duguid prepared some on philosophy and strategy. They organized the clinic at the Granite Club, and opened it to both male and female students, but as it turned out no men registered for it.

The clinic was a success, so Duguid, Turnbull and Ursuliak held others, in Calgary and Edmonton, in that same season. By the time the Canadian Ladies' Championship was held in 1969, women curlers across the country had heard good things about the instructional clinics, so in 1969–70 about twenty were arranged; in 1970–71 there were close to fifty. Eventually, schools were held in all except two Canadian provinces.

By 1971 Sven Eklund of Sweden's curling association had heard of the DTU schools, and of course he was also aware that at this time Don Duguid's was the biggest name in the sport. He arranged to have a clinic in his country in 1971–72. As events turned out, Duguid decided not to go to Sweden, but Eklund informed Turnbull that he wanted the clinic even though the star attraction wasn't available. Duguid was already doing colour commentary on televised curling games, and he wasn't enthusiastic about travelling nearly half-way around the world to teach. Within a couple of years he dropped out of the partnership with Turnbull and Ursuliak.

Turnbull and Ursuliak were extremely nervous before they put on their first clinic in Sweden, because they could tell that their students were highly motivated. But the Swedes were not hard to impress because when it came to curling they were in the Dark Ages, which is to say, the nineteenth century. Their fundamentals were weak and they had no sense of strategy. They were happy with the clinic – confident they would improve if they applied the ideas their instructors had offered. Turnbull and Ursuliak conducted two more clinics in Sweden that same year.

One of the students at the original Stockholm clinic was Roberto Carragatti, a member of the executive of the curling association in Switzerland. He persuaded other members of his association that Swiss curlers would benefit if they attended the type of school he just had. The next year, 1972–73, Turnbull and Ursuliak instructed for the first time in Switzerland. From that country they arranged clinics in Norway and Denmark. By the mid-1970s Turnbull, Ursuliak and their instructors annually were teaching hundreds of Europeans how to play the game. In the late 1970s, Ursuliak began to distance himself from the European operations in order to concentrate on promoting curling in Japan. Turnbull soon purchased Ursuliak's interest in the European operation, and through 1986–87 he continued to spend at least part of each curling season there.

Over the course of seventeen years, Turnbull, and sometimes Ursuliak, taught world men's champion skips Kjell Oscarius and Ragnar Kamp of Sweden, Kristian Soerum and Eigil Ramsfjell of Norway, and Otto Danielli of Switzerland, not to mention most of the members on their championship teams. Turnbull, Ursuliak and their staff also taught world women's champions Elizabeth Hogstrom of Sweden and Marianne Jorgensen of Denmark. In fact the Turnbull group taught most of Europe's

Don Duguid's tuck delivery

Pat Ryan's tuck delivery, developed in
Manitoba

Mike Riley's delivery, half-way between
flat-foot and tuck

best curlers. Turnbull and his staff took immense pride in being well prepared and enthusiastic, and they were successful teachers largely because they possessed these qualities. It was also true, as Otto Danielli says and Turnbull freely admits, that these students "worked like crazy" at the sport, sometimes for four or five hours a day in the curling season.[21]

Winnipeg was still a special curling city, then, partly because of what some Winnipeg people continued to accomplish as curlers, and partly because of what others did or had done to develop excellent curlers throughout Canada and the world. It was also a special place because of the treatment the sport received from members of the media there. Winnipeg reporters continued to cover curling extensively, and Winnipeg technicians and producers developed many of the procedures used to televise it.

By the 1950s, G.M. "Scotty" Harper of the *Free Press* had become the most famous curling reporter in Canada. He wrote about the roarin' game until he died in 1969, but long before that his curling columns were supplemented by features written by Maurice Smith. Smith was sports editor of the newspaper from 1946 to 1976. He went to the Brier nearly every year, and wrote about curling almost daily for a week or more from the site of the event. He also frequently offered opinions or information on curling throughout the winter. He was very much aware of happenings in the sport, not least because his wife, Nan, was of Scottish origin and was an enthusiastic curler in the Deer Lodge Ladies' Club.

In the 1950s Smith hired Don Blanchard, who began to cover major curling events as well as baseball and football, and who eventually succeeded Harper as the main curling reporter. Blanchard was a much more polished and fluent writer than either Harper or Smith were. He enjoyed the game and the people in it, and this showed in his columns. In 1971 he became the first recipient of the Scotty Harper Memorial Award, presented by the Canadian Curling Reporters for the best story on the sport.

By the time Blanchard left the *Free Press* late in the 1970s, Barbara Huck and Ralph Bagley had been writing about the sport for some time. Huck in particular wrote intriguing feature stories before she moved out of sports, and in 1983 won a Scotty Harper memorial award for a story on Ray Turnbull. Huck and Bagley were assigned their tasks by Hal Sigurdson, the man who succeeded Maurice Smith as sports editor. He was not as enthusiastic about curling as Smith had been, and he was aware that administrators of several amateur sports were jealous of the amount of coverage curling had received over the years. But he knew that both Ralph Bagley and many of his readers loved the sport, and Sigurdson continued to have major curling events covered as well as, if not better than, they were covered by other major dailies across the country.[22]

Jack Matheson wrote about curling – or at least the major events in curling – for the *Winnipeg Tribune*, the major competitor of the *Free Press*, from the mid-1950s until his newspaper folded in 1980. He did this well enough to win three Scotty Harper awards. Matheson was in his early twenties when he joined the *Trib* in 1946. One of his first assignments was to interview Jimmy Welsh, Brier champion in 1947. He came away from the interview intrigued and impressed by Welsh's combined humility and dedication to excellence. He had the same reaction when he met Bill Walsh a few years later, and once Matheson began to cover curling regularly he discovered that, on balance, he liked competitive curlers better than he liked athletes in any other sport. He also liked the people who organized and followed curling. "They wear too many badges, and they hold too many meetings and they stay up too late" – all of this was true. They also drank too much, but they

114

didn't become violent. This was refreshing to a man who went to the Grey Cup every year, an event that attracted the "punk element" and where parties ended with "furniture . . . wrecked and thrown out 19th-storey windows." Matheson also discovered, as countless reporters have, that administrators of the Brier and other important curling events assisted members of the media and accommodated both their needs and their idiosyncrasies to a degree that administrators of events in other sports did not.

Matheson admits now that, especially in the 1960s and 1970s when he and Don Blanchard were two of the best sportswriters in Canada, the two Winnipeg newspapers gave too much coverage to curling. But the reporters and editors were afraid they might lose readers if they cut back. Besides, for both Blanchard and Matheson, there were so many marvellous athletic performances in curling, and so many great people with whom one could sit around and laugh and tell stories.[23]

The Winnipeg electronic media also had a special relationship with curling. Certain private local radio stations covered the sport at least as extensively as any other in Canada did. This was the case in the 1940s, 1950s and 1960s at CJRC (now CKRC) and then CKY when "Cactus" Jack Wells was in his prime and had a close relationship with the MacDonald Tobacco Company. It became true of CJOB in the mid-1960s, when Bob Picken became OB's first full-time sports director. It remained true of CJOB after Picken was succeeded by Ken Nicholson and Bob Irving; in the late-1980s CJOB was one of the few private stations in Canada that still was willing to pay for sending their own reporters to cover major national and international curling events. Meanwhile, on the national CBC radio network, Bill Good of Winnipeg had been part of the two-man announcing team that in 1946 did the first live country-wide broadcasts of the Brier. From that point, until early in the 1980s, the CBC usually chose Winnipeg-based broadcasters such as Bob Willson and, after 1969, Bob Picken, to go to the Brier site to provide a certain amount of play-by-play as well as extensive summaries of happenings in different draws.[24]

In television, local stations such as CBWT, CKY (formerly CJAY), and CKND always paid a great deal of attention to curling. Sometimes one of them carried live broadcasts of the provincial championship event; in fact in the late 1980s the arrangement between CKND and the MCA to televise key games in Manitoba's Labatt Tankard Playdowns was believed to be unique in the sport. Furthermore, Winnipeggers such as Don Wittman and Don Duguid were usually the "voices" of curling on the CBC national network, and the executives of that network who fought hardest to put curling programs on the air and to keep them there were Winnipeggers, or former Winnipeggers such as Gordon Craig. When Craig moved from the CBC in 1982 to become president of The Sports Network (TSN), one of the convictions he took with him was that curling could be an important and attractive part of his new network's programming. Since 1984, when TSN went on the air, the ratings that have been taken indicate that his instincts were sound. The popularity of curling on TSN is attributable in large part to the lucid, informed colour commentary provided by Ray Turnbull.[25]

Craig started working on sports as a technician at CBWT, the CBC station in Winnipeg. The production crews at this station really pioneered most of the techniques used to do play-by-play coverage of curling. Late in the 1950s those crews filmed an invitational tournament at the Granite Curling Club and showed it locally. In the 1960s what had become a local curling show developed into the weekly Cross Canada Curling and then the CBC Curling Classic, shown by the full network and featuring big-name national

Maurice Smith

Don Blanchard

Ralph Bagley

Jack Matheson (right)

"Cactus" Jack Wells

Jack Wells and "Leslie Wells Singers" entertain at media gathering, 1970 Silver Broom, Utica

Don Wittman (left) and Bob Picken (right)

Ray Turnbull (right) with fellow TSN commentators Vic Rauter and Linda Moore

Scene from 1952 Brier in Amphitheatre

Scene from 1970 Brier, Winnipeg Arena

Scene of crowd watching action at the 1975 Canadian Mixed Championship at St. Vital Curling Club

and international teams competing for cash prizes. The weekly show was produced out of Winnipeg until 1979–80, with the exception of three years late in the 1960s. Meanwhile, Winnipeg crews under the direction of producers George Kent and Leo Hebert began to cover the Brier and other major events regularly for the CBC. As a result of all the time they spent on curling, they developed most of the procedures and equipment that were later adopted by others to cover the sport. These included a camera on wheels following rocks down the ice, lights placed along the length of the curling sheet, a telestrator with which the colour commentator could diagram shots, and wireless microphones placed on the curlers themselves. It is not too much to say that Winnipeggers created most of the special means that will be used to televise curling through the rest of the twentieth century.[26]

Another reason Winnipeg remained a special place was that in the 1960s, 1970s and 1980s Winnipeg curlers and the two curling organizations with headquarters in Winnipeg became world renowned as hosts of major curling events. In the 1950s, the reputation of Winnipeg and the MCA in this regard had declined. In 1952, the city and the organization hosted the Brier for the second time at the Amphitheatre. The event was administered capably. The only problem was that only about 12,500 people attended, and by this time total attendance for the week-long tournament had topped 20,000 in three different cities. Then in 1957, a national schoolboys' championship took place in the Winnipeg Arena, which was constructed just two years earlier in the west end of the city proper, close to St. James. This tournament too failed to draw the crowds expected. In both 1952 and 1957, potential groups of spectators were ignored or alienated through inadequate promotion or inappropriate ticket prices.[27]

In the next three decades, however, Winnipeggers arranged a number of successful events. Different individual clubs in the city, with the cooperation of the MCA, the MLCA, or both, hosted three mixed, four junior and three senior national championships. In 1968, 1976 and 1985, Winnipeg was the site of three of the finest Canadian women's championships in history; in two of the three years, attendance records were set.[28] The 1970 Brier was held at the Winnipeg Arena, and it was the most successful Brier ever held to that point. During the first day, some of the normal problems involved in creating keen ice in a warm arena had to be solved by ice maker Andy McWilliams, but thereafter the playing conditions were excellent. More than 60,000 fans attended in total, which was about 8,000 more than had attended the 1965 Brier in Saskatoon, where the previous record had been established. A single-game attendance record of 9,438 was established. It still stands.[29] A few minutes before the final draw began, radio stations in Winnipeg had to inform listeners that if they were driving to the Arena expecting to buy tickets they might as well turn around and go home: the place was sold out.[30]

The biggest curling event Winnipeggers ever hosted was the 1978 Silver Broom. It was also the biggest sports event in the city since the 1967 Pan-American Games, and it still enjoys that distinction. It generated a $110,000 profit which, along with the interest, is still being used for the benefit of curling. Over 102,000 spectators came to the twelve different draws at the 1978 event. This is still a record for total attendance at the world men's championship. The opening ceremony was an unprecedented spectacle of colour, sound and pageantry that celebrated the ethnic history of Manitoba. Each of the ten competing nations was honoured at a draw; the country's national anthem was played, its curlers received gifts, and its flag was raised. Teams, fans and members of the international media were hosted at "ethnic" nights at different city curling clubs. In fact the city's clubs stopped their regular activities for the whole week in order to entertain guests. A huge banquet was arranged at Winnipeg's new downtown Convention Centre. Approximately 3,000 people attended. One of them was Don Turner of Weyburn, Saskatchewan. Turner says that when the caterers turned out the lights, and the waitresses brought cakes with candles on them into the room for dessert, it was one of the most fantastic sights he'd ever witnessed. He does not hesitate to say that the Winnipeg Silver Broom was the best world championship curling event in history, and he has been to several of them. His opinion is shared by many, and perhaps most, of the hundreds of people who attend world championships regularly.[31] This is the main reason they look forward to the 1991 combined World Men's and Ladies' championships to be held in Winnipeg, which probably will be another milestone event.

Over the years, there were a few Winnipeg people, officers of the MCA and the MLCA, who could take some credit for the successful national championship events held in rural Manitoba – the junior men's championship at Flin Flon in 1967; the combined senior men's and senior women's championship at Portage la Prairie in 1986; the 1963 and 1982 Briers held in Brandon, the 1982 Brier being the first one to draw over 100,000 fans.[32] But local organizers are always the key to hosting successful curling championships, and ultimately Winnipeggers can be given credit only for the events in their own city. Hundreds of different individuals sacrificed time and money to make the Winnipeg events memorable. The key people were veterans at organizing events at the club, zone and provincial levels. Among the women were Joan Whalley, Marion Lynch, Edith Tipping and Ina Light; among the men were Bob Picken, Cec Watt, Vic Palmer and Lorne Cameron. Two of the important con-

tributors were a man and a woman who were, respectively, the most renowned male and female administrators of curling in Manitoba, and perhaps in Canada, in the post–Second World War years. Both of them came from the Elmwood Curling Club, and both of them served their national curling associations as president in the same year.

The man was Bill Lumsden. Lumsden was born in Brandon in 1907 but moved to Winnipeg as a youngster. He began to curl at the Elmwood Club in the 1920s, and became secretary in 1934 and president in 1939. He was an MCA officer for twenty-nine years and president of the association in 1947–48. He was a fine orator and a man who made it a point to recognize the contributions that "little" people made to successful curling clubs or events – hospitality-room workers, volunteer car drivers, and the like. In the 1960s, he became a member of the executive of the CCA and moved through the ranks to become president in 1967–68. He may have been the most effective executive officer in the CCA's history. He was instrumental in establishing a national senior men's championship and in obtaining a sponsor for it. He helped persuade Air Canada to become sponsor of the world men's championship in 1968, after the Scotch Whisky Association had decided they no longer wanted to be involved. In committee rooms he fought and often won noteworthy battles: against establishing a "code of ethics" that would have made curlers who won expensive prizes at bonspiels ineligible for national championships; for a change in name from DCA to CCA; for the selection of a Brier site two years in advance rather than one; for allowing a fifth man on teams in national championships so that there would be a substitute available in case of injury or illness to a regular member; for the rule change that allowed one-sided games to be terminated any time after eight ends if the weaker team so desired. (It is no

*Closing ceremonies, 1976 Canadian La-
dies' Championship, Winnipeg Arena*

Scenes from 1978 Silver Broom, Winnipeg Arena

125

Edith Tipping

Joan Whalley

Cec Watt

Bill Lumsden

longer necessary to wait until the eighth end to terminate a one-sided game.) Between 1969, his last year as an executive of the national curling organization, and 1982, when he died, he dedicated his energy again to Manitoba and Winnipeg curling affairs. His most important contributions were made as chair of the MCA's organizing committee for the Brier in 1970; at that event, he even sang the national anthem at the opening ceremonies because of a technical problem with the recorded music. He was also chair of the Ethnic Entertainment Committee for the 1978 Silver Broom.[33]

Lumsden's female counterpart was Lura McLuckie. She was born Lura Price in 1912. Her father and mother were charter members of the Elmwood Curling Club and Elmwood Ladies' Curling Club, respectively; Lura grew up around the Elmwood building and threw her first curling rocks there. In 1929 she joined the Eaton Ladies' Curling Club but came back to the Elmwood in 1938 after she married Alex McLuckie. She held a number of executive positions in the club and was president in 1949–50. Later she became involved in the administration of the MLCA, and served as secretary for two years in the mid-1950s, then as president in 1962–63.

In February 1960, McLuckie was the Manitoba delegate to the organizational meeting of the CLCA held in Toronto. She became first vice-president of the association in 1966–67 and president in 1967–68. During these two years she made her enviable national and international reputation as an administrator. As it happened, in 1966–67, the Southern Ontario Ladies' Curling Association wanted to change the way the CLCA operated. They did not think each province, no matter how big or small, should have equal voting power. In other words, they wanted their own huge association to have more clout. They were supported by Dominion Stores Limited, the company that had sponsored the Canadian Ladies' Championship event since 1961 when it began. McLuckie used her influence to ensure that the CLCA remained an organization in which each province had equal strength. This caused the temporary withdrawal of the Southern Ontario Association from the CLCA and the loss of support from Dominion Stores for the national championship.

In the next year, 1967–68, McLuckie was president of the CLCA and was faced with the job of putting on a national championship in Winnipeg without the help of a sponsor. She and a strong local committee headed by Joan Whalley of the Deer Lodge Club worked like demons, and they arranged the best women's championship event ever held to that point. Mabel Mitchell of Brandon was the skip of the rink that represented Manitoba in that championship. She remembers walking onto the ice for the opening ceremony at the St. James Civic Centre. Tears came to her eyes. There was a pipe band, and the stands were full of people! She had curled in important women's events where the spectators were outnumbered by the participants. Here she was at a women's championship that featured all the pomp and ceremony and crowd enthusiasm of a major men's event. To Mitchell, it seemed that women's curling had come of age. The whole tournament was administered splendidly, and the total attendance of approximately 11,000 established a record.

McLuckie remains to this day an enthusiastic worker on behalf of women's curling. She made an important contribution to Winnipeg's reputation as a host city not only through her work on the 1968 Canadian Ladies' Championship, but also through efforts made to make the 1970 Brier and 1978 Silver Broom successful. She was on a committee in both years; in fact in 1978 she was the secretary on Bill Lumsden's Ethnic Entertainment Committee.[34]

The provincial curling associations over which Lumsden and McLuckie once presided, the MCA and MLCA, respectively, were consistently the second, third or fourth largest men's or women's curling associations in the country. They were still growing in membership in the late-1950s and continued to do so until the early to mid-1960s. Then the curling boom that had begun in the 1940s dissipated, and membership either declined or levelled off. The clubs in the MCA had a total of just over 17,000 members in 1959–60. Over the next five years, total membership declined by about 1,500, but then went back up to more than 17,000 in 1966–67. Thereafter it steadily dropped to just below 14,000 by early in the 1980s, and it remained at 14,000 to 15,000 thereafter.[35] The MLCA clubs had had only about 500 members by the mid-1930s and about 1,300 by the mid-1940s, but had some 5,300 members by 1959–60 and over 7,800 by 1965–66. Over the next twenty years, membership grew slowly to just under 10,000.[36]

In the 1970s the officers of the MCA and MLCA became uneasy about the club membership figures, as well as by other statistics that suggested curling was not as popular as it once had been among teenagers and young adults. Perhaps the officers were overly concerned. The patterns in the numbers of members possessed by Manitoba clubs – growth from the 1940s to the 1960s, then decline or stabilization – were common across the country. Furthermore, membership statistics did not identify the vast majority of casual curlers, and there were thousands of these. This was revealed in a 1981 Canada fitness survey which showed that 17.8 percent of all Manitobans over the age of ten, or some 155,00 people, had curled at least once in the previous twelve months; this was just slightly below the number and percentage in Saskatchewan, but far ahead of the number and percentage in other provinces. Still, the figures and the

impressions possessed by the officers of the two Manitoba associations suggested some action should be taken. In 1980 the MCA established a task force on junior curling that promoted interest in the sport by making school presentations and by helping to create a short film entitled "The Curling Touch," designed for young audiences. In 1985 the men's and women's associations jointly hired a full-time technical director, Patti Vandekerckhove (Patti Vande), the first curling technical director in the country whose job description included promotion of the sport. In 1986, with government assistance provided through the Manitoba Sports Federation and its gaming fund, an organization called Results Group was hired to conduct a survey of the state of curling in the province. Results Group concluded that curling had an image problem among non-curlers – the sport was perceived as slow, boring and unathletic. Soon the curling associations produced television commercials that featured attractive male and female teenagers and young adults who possessed smooth curling deliveries and who had all kinds of fun and good times after their games. In 1988 it appeared that these initiatives were having a positive effect, but it was really too early to tell.[37]

The decline in the number of members was not as pronounced as was the decline in the number of clubs. This fact was not revealed in the MLCA because there "clubs" were in effect "leagues": this meant that in 1986–87, for example, there were three women's clubs in Gimli, the Monday Night, Wednesday Night and Ladies Afternoon clubs.[38] In the MCA, however, a "club" was an organization that operated a curling building, or which once had operated a building and retained membership in the MCA on the approval of its executive council.[39] In the MCA there were 316 clubs in 1959–60, but only 233 by 1976–77 and 192 by 1985–86.[40]

Lura McLuckie

Patti Vande

Connie Laliberte delivering rock

Patti Vande and Chris Pidzarko demonstrate athletic sweeping

In the 1960s, 1970s and 1980s, a few new clubs were formed, it is true. These appeared mostly in towns and cities in the northern part of the province – in Churchill, for example, or Gillam, Leaf Rapids or Norway House. They appeared as well in rural communities such as St. Adolphe, Lorette or Vita, where a large number of French Canadians, Ukrainians, Poles or another ethnic group were still picking up the sport.[41] However, the number of new clubs formed was vastly outnumbered by old ones that folded. They disappeared especially in smaller agricultural service centres. If the members were not sufficiently numerous or affluent to put in artificial ice they disbanded and joined a club in a larger community nearby. Developments in the Brandon-Souris district are instructive. In 1957–58, there were clubs in Alexander, Carroll, Elgin, Fairfax, Justice, Kemnay, Margaret and Minto, but in 1986–87 all of them were defunct.[42]

In Winnipeg, the numbers of "city" clubs in the MCA was twenty in 1957–58 and twenty-three in 1986–87. Actually, only two new clubs were formed in the city, the Rossmere and the Wildewood. Each had been founded originally as a golf or country club, the former in 1950, the latter in 1930. They added curling to their activities in 1959 and 1962, respectively. In doing so they acted as a large number of eastern Canadian golf and country clubs did in the 1950s and 1960s.[43] However, the formation of the two new clubs was more than balanced by the amalgamation of the two military clubs into CFB Winnipeg in 1968–69, along with the termination of the Eaton Club in 1975 and the Strathcona Club in 1982.[44] To see the Strathcona Club, the old "home of champions," cease operations was particularly troubling for Manitoba curlers. Meanwhile, the Highlander Club came and went in the 1960s.[45] The greater number of Winnipeg clubs that existed in the late 1980s compared to the late 1950s is accounted for by the designation of suburban clubs or clubs located just outside Winnipeg as "city" rather than "rural" ones. Organizations that had been rural but became city were the Assiniboine-Memorial, the Charleswood and the Transcona clubs. The West St. Paul Club formed in 1962 also was designated a city club.[46]

It made good sense to label the Charleswood, Assiniboine-Memorial and Transcona clubs as city organizations, of course, because by the 1960s Winnipeg and its suburbs represented a metropolitan district of about half a million people, and the introduction of a Metro Government in 1960 and then the formation of Unicity in 1972 meant that the three clubs were located in Greater Winnipeg.[47] It also made sense to call the West St. Paul Club a city club, because many of its members came from Winnipeg. The same was true of the East St. Paul, Domain, La Salle, Stony Mountain, Lorette and other clubs located just outside the Perimeter Highway.[48] Perhaps the city members joined one of these "rural" clubs because they had friends or relatives in the "bedroom community" in which they curled. Perhaps, too, the city members had been born in the small centres and liked to drive "home" once or twice a week. Finally, perhaps they couldn't join a city club located near them.

Most of the Winnipeg clubs did not have room for large numbers of new members, and no new clubs were formed in the city after 1962. The commercial, or "other," rates at which curling clubs were taxed by the City of Winnipeg made it difficult if not impossible to expand or build anew. The Granite Club, which had managed to buy its property back from the Government of Manitoba in 1946 after thirty years as a tenant, decided in 1975 not to pay taxes that had accumulated for three or four years, but to sell its property to the city and rent it back. Representatives of the MCA made frequent appeals to the city and provincial governments to reduce curling-club taxes to the residential rate, or even to eliminate them altogether. Those representatives had not managed to obtain the desired results by 1988. City officials were sympathetic to the curling clubs' problems, but asked how they would lower the taxes on curling clubs without lowering them also on bowling alleys, pool rooms, even amusement centres. The MCA's people could not answer the question to the city's aatisfaction.[49]

The number of members in Winnipeg's men's clubs went from about 5,600 to 6,100 between the mid-1960s and the mid-1970s, and then levelled off.[50] The number of women in curling clubs went from about 1,450 in 1959–60 to about 3,320 in 1985–86.[51] Most of the women's clubs were, in effect, leagues that rented ice. There were dozens of rental leagues formed by men as well. This meant renters became far more numerous and visible around the curling clubs than they had been thirty or forty years earlier. The artificial ice and the lounges the clubs installed were expensive to maintain, the taxes were hard to pay, and some of the regular members did not want to play as many times per week over a five- or six-month season as they had over a three- or four-month one. Renting the ice more frequently represented an adaptation to a number of changed circumstances.[52]

Curling was now a sport played by people of both genders, of nearly all ages and income groups. It was also played in large numbers by people of British background, of course, and by descendants of the continental Europeans who had come to Canada and the West before 1930. In 1974–75 the list of regular members of the Elmwood Curling Club included several Mennonite, Polish, Ukrainian and Jewish names. The names of the curlers who represented Manitoba in national men's, women's and mixed championships also suggested the degree to which people of central or northern European background

had taken up the sport – Braunstein, Lerner, Meleschuk, Finkbeiner, Burtnyk, Gunnlaugson, Hildebrand, Bradawaski, Pidzarko, Tanasichuk.[53] However, among the ethnic groups who migrated to the city in large numbers only after the 1950s, there were hardly any curlers. Certain Europeans such as the Portuguese, the Asians, South Americans and West Indians were unfamiliar with curling when they arrived, and they remained unfamiliar with it thereafter because the curling clubs and associations in Winnipeg did not promote the game among them. This was one reason the Civic-Caledonian and other clubs located in neighbourhoods where the new immigrants were numerous were in financial difficulty.[54]

Among the members of clubs and many of the renters, the calibre of play improved immensely between the 1950s and the 1980s. Every curling club in the city installed artificial ice in the 1950s or early 1960s. The advent of artificial ice plus the matched rocks available since the 1940s worked together to make conditions of play much more consistent. The evolution of sliding materials also had a positive effect on the quality of curling. In the 1950s most curlers either still threw from the hack in a stand-up style or slipped off one toe rubber as Ken Watson had done in order to slide. Some of them, however, were beginning to apply liquid solder to the sole of their sliding shoe in order to cut down on friction. In the late 1950s and in the 1960s they substituted a piece of teflon for the liquid solder, and in the 1970s and 1980s they purchased manufactured curling shoes with brick or even stainless steel on the bottom. The innovations in footwear made it easier to develop smooth exits from the hack and reasonably sound deliveries.[55]

The main factor in the improvement of the players, however, was the development of instructional clinics. The MCA and some of its member clubs began to hold these regularly in the mid-1960s.[56] Later in that decade, Don Duguid, Ray Turnbull and Wally Ursuliak began their successful clinics. Then in 1974, Curl Canada was established. Curl Canada is financed by the federal government through the National Coaches' Certification Program. It now offers clinics on making ice, on managing clubs and on officiating, but its initial purpose is still its most important purpose: to instruct curlers and the coaches of curlers in the fundamental skills of the sport and in the elements of strategy. Curl Canada's instruction program followed closely the program that Duguid-Turnbull-Ursuliak had developed in the late 1960s and early 1970s; of course the DTU program incorporated ideas and practices that good curlers had utilized for decades. The full-time technical director of Curl Canada from 1980 to 1986 was Garry DeBlonde. He had been one of Winnipeg's top curlers in the 1960s and 1970s. He was a member of two Canadian mixed champion teams and two Manitoba Brier representatives. He and his brother, Clare, were gentlemanly but slow players; Don Turner of Weyburn half-jokingly says that the DeBlonde's lengthy games at the Regina Brier of 1976 were the reason Brier games were reduced from twelve to ten ends in 1977. Through the clinics arranged by Garry DeBlonde and his predecessors, and especially through ongoing assistance provided at the club level from certified instructors, literally thousands of Manitoba and Canadian curlers improved their skills in the 1970s and 1980s.[57]

Improvement in the level of play was particularly evident in women's curling. In the 1950s there were still many women – some of them considered competent curlers – who placed both feet in the hack, who slid on their knees when they threw the rock, and who backed down the ice as they swept a stone. But by the 1970s and 1980s, women curled with considerable skill. They sometimes came out of the hack with powerful and truly beautiful sliding deliveries, and they swept rhythmically and effectively.[58]

Women benefitted from better ice, better shoes and, especially because they were usually more willing than men to be coached, better instruction. It was also true that their sweeping compared more favourably to men's sweeping after the mid-1970s, when horse-hair "push" brooms were adopted by Canadian curlers, because these brooms rewarded sheer strength and endurance less than the earlier corn "swish" broom did. Just as important as all these factors to improvement in women's curling, however, was the change in attitude of the women who played the sport. In the 1960s, 1970s and 1980s, they were more aggressive and more competitive than the female curlers of earlier generations. In Winnipeg, as in all of Canada and virtually the whole western world, after the 1950s, women were working more and more outside the home, had independent incomes, and demanded political rights and social privileges to an extent they never had previously. They asserted themselves on the curling ice as well as in offices or legislatures. They took pride in their athletic ability and it showed in the way they performed on the ice as well as on the golf course, tennis court, ball diamond, ski slope or rifle range. In the late 1980s, top women curlers were not as good at sweeping as the top men were, but they were nearly as good at throwing rocks. This certainly had not been the case in the 1950s.[59]

The greater overall skill of curlers was revealed in particular at the annual MCA Bonspiel. Individuals who had participated in or watched bonspiel games in the 1930s and 1940s could hardly believe the quality of shot-making they witnessed in the 1980s.[60] Yet it was not the calibre of play in it that made the bonspiel a main reason Winnipeg was still a special place in curling. It was the size of it, and the atmosphere surrounding it.

Annual entries in the regular events of the bonspiel increased from 368 rinks to 468 between 1957 and 1962, then shot up to 680 for the seventy-fifth-anniversary bonspiel in 1963. Entries dropped gradually thereafter to 323 teams in 1966, the lowest since 1943. At this point the MCA officials adopted a new format that had been discussed for many years. They opened the bonspiel on a Thursday, not a Monday or Tuesday. They also initiated Sunday curling. These departures, together with the one taken in 1958 that erased one open event on each side of the "string," made it possible to have most teams eliminated from competition by Sunday night. The majority of rural curlers were required now to be away from home only four days, not seven or eight. The majority of urban curlers had to miss only one or two days of work. The better teams then played their semi-final and final games in the different events from Monday through Wednesday.[61]

The new format was an immediate success. In 1967, the first year it was used, there were 496 entries, fifty percent more than there were in the previous year. By 1970 there were over 500 entries, and two years later the MCA had to place a ceiling on the number of rinks allowed to compete. The limit went from 536 in 1972 to 728 by 1976, and to 848 by 1985. For the hundredth-anniversary bonspiel in 1988, there were 1,280 teams allowed to enter, and play began on the Wednesday, but in 1989 the Thursday opening and an 848-team limit were reinstated.[62]

Meanwhile, in 1966, a second event for older curlers was inaugurated. One became eligible for the two events at age fifty-five; previously, to enter the single veteran's event a curler had to be sixty. A few years later the two events for men fifty-five and over became a "senior's" event for those fifty and over, and a "master's" event for those who were at least sixty. In the 1950s the one competition for older curlers drew two- or three-dozen teams, but by the mid-1970s the two events together attracted about 100 entries, and in 1986 they had 120.[63]

The seniors' and veterans' events always opened after most of the teams in the regular men's bonspiel had been eliminated. So did the MLCA Bonspiel, for which the MCA administered the draws. The women's bonspiel had 100 to 150 rinks in the 1930s, and 150 to 200 in the 1960s and early 1970s. In the late 1970s, an adjusted format was introduced that created in effect two bonspiels and made it easier for women to enter and still meet their commitments to jobs and families. An event for women sixty years of age and over was added. The total number of entries, however, remained in the 160 to 200 range.[64]

The MCA Bonspiel, then, was really three bonspiels, and the number of teams climbed to the remarkable total of 1,576 in 1988.[65] Keeping track of all the teams and what transpired in their games was the responsibility of the MCA's Bonspiel Committee – and its computer, first used to monitor some events in 1975, and used for the whole bonspiel in 1985.[66] The capable and immensely dedicated secretaries and executive director of the association, Vic Siddall from 1952 to 1966, Alex Williamson from 1966 to 1983, and Lorne Kingyens thereafter, became less and less involved in the bonspiel. They were preoccupied with keeping track of the day-to-day affairs of an association that organized or supervised more and more competitions and that had a total budget of some $50,000 in 1962, $225,000 in 1982–83 and $450,000 in 1986–87.[67]

The Bonspiel Committee and the computer were faced with entries whose numbers increased much faster than did the number of sheets of ice in the city to accommodate games. This is why the limitation on

Don Duguid's front end works corn brooms, 1970

Mike Riley's front end brushing the rock that won the Brier, 1984

entries had to be instituted early in the 1970s. In 1959 the bonspiel organizers utilized 102 sheets of ice available through Winnipeg's curling clubs. They also used five sheets in the Winnipeg Arena for a few days. In that year they chose not to schedule games in the facilities of the Assiniboine Memorial, Transcona and Charleswood clubs, which then had a total of thirteen sheets.[68] In 1987, bonspiel organizers utilized 172 sheets of ice, but twenty-eight of them in total were located in East St. Paul, Springfield, Stony Mountain, St. Adolphe, La Salle, Selkirk, Lorette and Rosser. There were 144 sheets available through Winnipeg clubs.[69] The Eaton and Strathcona clubs were gone by this time, of course, and with them went a total of ten sheets. The two military clubs in 1959 had a total of seven sheets; in 1987 the CFB Club had only four sheets because a fire had damaged its old RCAF Westwin Building. The Fort Garry and St. Vital clubs had new buildings at their old locations with the same six sheets that each of the old structures had possessed. Of the fifty-five new sheets, twelve came with the six-sheet buildings the Rossmere and Wildewood clubs built, respectively, at Watt and Leighton and on North Drive. Four more came with the West St. Paul Club's building located just west of Main Street and north of the Perimeter Highway. New eight-sheet structures were put up in 1972 by the Assiniboine Memorial Club at Vimy and Hamilton, and by the Transcona Club at Plessis Road and Highway 15; this added sixteen sheets because the eight the old buildings had contained were not used in 1959. The Charleswood Club's five-sheet rink was utilized in 1987 but not in 1959. In 1958–59 the Fort Rouge Club was renting ice from the Granite Club. The Fort Rouge Club's new building on Daly Street opened in 1959–60 with six sheets that were still available in 1987. The Heather Club's new eight-sheet rink on Youville was one sheet

larger than its former facility on Braemar was. The Winter Club added four sheets at its building in 1966. The Maple Leaf Club sold its five-sheet building on Machray Avenue in 1970, but it rented six sheets at the Highlander Complex on Ellice Avenue, and these were utilized. The Highlander building was erected in 1964 and contained bays of ice that could be used for hockey or curling; in 1987 six sheets were used for the bonspiel in addition to the six rented for the year by the Maple Leaf Club.[70]

The percentage of rural teams in the bonspiel was never as high from the 1950s through the 1980s as it had been in the 1930s and 1940s. It is clear that in the 1950s and early 1960s this had something to do with the greater resentment rural that curlers felt toward Winnipeggers than they had felt at any time previously. They were concerned that the MCA was run by Winnipeg curlers primarily for their own benefit. By the mid-1960s, animosity had reached such great levels that there were advocates of a second curling association in the northwest part of the province, and in 1966 there were only ninety-seven rural teams entered in the bonspiel, the lowest total since 1934.[71]

Already by the mid-1960s the MCA was taking overdue steps to address the concerns of rural members, and soon it took even more. In 1960 the organization held its semi-annual meeting outside Winnipeg for the first time. This precedent was followed thereafter. In 1962–63, representatives of rural clubs began to be elected to the MCA Council, and in 1974–75 Jim Wishart of Portage la Prairie became the first rural president of the body. In 1966 the Consols were held in Dauphin, the first occasion on which it was played outside Winnipeg. The intention was to alternate between rural and Winnipeg sites for the event. This plan was abandoned eventually, but the Consols, which became the Labatt Tankard Playdowns in 1980, continued to be held regularly in centres other than Winnipeg.

All of these initiatives and others helped ease the tensions between rural and urban curlers, as increased rural entries in the bonspiel in the late 1960s indicated.[72]

Early in the 1970s, when limitations were placed on the number of rinks allowed in the bonspiel, one-quarter of the spots were reserved for non-Winnipeg entries. Thereafter, one-quarter to one-third were set aside. Since the amount of total entries kept increasing, so did the number of rural teams: there were 176 in 1976, 190 in 1980 and 210 in 1986.[73] Because the number of rural Manitobans as well as the number of rural Manitoba curlers actually declined between the mid-1960s and the mid-1980s,[74] the increasing amount of entries from country rinks suggested renewed attachment to the bonspiel on the part of rural members of the MCA.

The circumstances under which rural teams came to the bonspiel were much different from what they once had been. Until the 1950s, rural curlers had come to the bonspiel during the slowest season of the agricultural year, and usually the rhythm of their lives had been dictated by agriculture even if they themselves were not farmers. Perhaps they had been joined by members of their families who came to Winnipeg on the train only once or twice a year and who wanted to shop and experience the cultural life of the city. After mid-century, rural curlers and rural people were not as directly affected by agriculture. They were more likely than ever before to be employed in the mining, energy or service sectors of the economy.[75] No matter what their occupation, most of them could jump in their cars and travel to Winnipeg at almost any time of the year. They did not come to the city primarily or only in winter, and a drastically reduced number of special bonspiel sales or theatrical productions was a consequence.

The rural Manitoba curlers were regularly accompanied to the bonspiel by a few rinks from other provinces, from the United States and even from Europe. Many of these teams came for the excellent competition the bonspiel offered. When someone like Otto Danielli, the Swiss curler who skipped the 1975 world-championship team, brought rinks to the bonspiel as he did on more than one occasion,[76] he did so partly because he knew he would meet as many tough teams in a week at Winnipeg as he might all year in Europe. But from the 1950s to the 1980s, the bonspiel became much more a social than a competitive curling event. In fact it became the biggest party in the sport.

By the 1950s, most Manitobans had become disenchanted with their restrictive liquor laws and regulations, and because the D.L. Campbell provincial government was aware of this fact it appointed a royal commission, chaired by former premier John Bracken, to report and advise it on changes that should occur in the liquor-control system. The commission recommended liberalization of drinking legislation. The Campbell government adopted its main suggestions and, as W.L. Morton put it, "local plebiscites" such as those held in Winnipeg and its suburbs "resulted in a widespread, almost general acceptance of some, or all, of the various ways which liquor might be sold to the public in hotels, restaurants, or other public resorts."[77] The availability of liquor licenses and the desire to install artificial ice explain the large number of new or renovated curling buildings that appeared between the mid-1950s and the mid-1960s. These facilities contained more cement and steel and less wood than did the rinks of earlier decades.[78] The licensed room was usually on the second floor of the building. Rather than offer their guests sips from a bottle in the basement "snake" room, club members now could treat them to a drink or two in the licensed lounge or dining room. Naturally they were inclined to do so during the bonspiel.

Alex Williamson

Otto Danielli

Then, in 1967, the adjusted bonspiel format was introduced. The new International Inn became headquarters for the event. It was the place where draws were made and results of games were charted. It became the site of the annual MCA smorgasbord or dinner which in the recent past had often been held at the Auditorium. The International Inn also was the location of most of the round-the-clock drinking and carousing that became associated with the bonspiel – at least the men's sections of it.

This drinking and carousing took place in private rooms rented by many rural curlers and even some city ones. It occurred also in the rooms rented by curling clubs, rooms that became gathering points for club members and their guests late at night or between draws. The club rooms might be small hospitality rooms where the drinks and snacks were free. More commonly they were larger conference-type rooms that contained a cash bar, that sometimes featured pornographic movies, and that almost always made tables available for card games. The atmosphere in these larger rooms was not unlike that at a stag party.

The rooms, and perhaps the drinks, were paid for through "calcuttas," which were started at most, if not all, city clubs in the late 1960s and early 1970s. Just where or when calcuttas originated is not known; several Winnipeg curlers recall seeing one for the first time at the British Consols held in Dauphin in 1966. Calcuttas were (and are) a form of lottery. Club members participated in an "auction" of the teams from the club in the bonspiel. They "bought" a team, and might or might not receive a payback, depending upon the performance of the squad they "owned." Calcuttas created heightened interest in the progress of teams from the club. They also generated revenue for the organization, because a certain percentage of the total amount bid on the teams went directly to the club.[79]

The curlers at the bonspiel followed a kind of code of honour which dictated that you showed up for your game no matter how much alcohol you had consumed or how bad you felt. No such code of honour obligated them to attend the annual bonspiel church service. By late in the 1960s, the curlers seemed to have no time or energy for church, and early in the 1970s the tradition disappeared.

The services had been declining in popularity for some time. Early in the twentieth century they had been an extremely important item on the bonspiel agenda; the churches in which they were held had been packed by curlers and their friends. By the 1930s, however, enthusiasm for the services was beginning to wane noticeably. In 1935 the MCA switched the time they were held from evening to morning, hoping especially to attract curlers from the country who sometimes were invited out for dinner on Sunday evening by city friends or relatives.[80] Altering the time had no effect; in the 1940s and 1950s, attendance continued to fall. In 1967, when Sunday draws were instituted, Sunday mornings were left free. But so few curlers were going to the services by this time that in 1971 they were discontinued as an official bonspiel function, and in 1973 Sunday morning draws were inaugurated.[81]

The bonspiel services declined in popularity primarily because the sermons that were featured in them became less and less relevant to the curlers. These sermons almost always were devoted to confirming in both curling and in life the value of concentration, discipline, teamwork, obedience and other qualities.[82] They had appealed to the early British-Protestant curlers who wanted to be reassured that their recreations were worthwhile and met with God's approval. By the 1950s and 1960s, a smaller proportion of curlers cared about God's opinion. Those who did seemed confident that God did not disapprove of the rush of pleasure stimulated by the well-played shot, by the witty remark, even by the occasional earthy joke.

Winning a major prize at the MCA Bonspiel was always a significant accomplishment from the 1950s to the 1980s. Moreover, there were always good teams that had to avoid the parties and make sure they played as well as they could because they had failed to qualify for the provincial championship through zone playdowns and had to do so through the bonspiel. For the great majority of curlers, however, the bonspiel represented a few days of fun, of story-telling, of renewing old friendships and creating new ones. As a competitive occasion, the bonspiel ranked far below the world, Canadian or provincial championship events, and even below some cash bonspiels. This fact was recognized in effect by the officials of the MCA when in 1977 they decided to stop charging admission to bonspiel finals.[83]

The bonspiel survived and grew from the 1950s through the 1980s because Manitoba's curlers chose to use it to emphasize the off-ice attractions of their sport. It is these attractions that recreational curlers from as far away as Alaska or continental Europe have in mind when they say that just once in their lives they would like to play in the greatest bonspiel in the world.[84] They think of Winnipeg as a special place. They would have different reasons for doing so if they were curling administrators, if they were competitive curlers or wanted to acquire the skills needed to excel at the sport, if they enjoyed watching competitive curling, or if they followed it closely through the mass media. No matter what aspect of curling they were particularly interested or involved in, something Winnipeggers had done or were doing would mean that for them, as for Rev. John Kerr back in 1903, Manitoba's capital had extraordinary significance.

Conclusion: A Hall of Fame

IN THE SPRING OF 1971, Noel Buxton of the Deer Lodge Curling Club became the president of the MCA. Buxton was like most presidents of most organizations in that he had a pet project on which he wanted to place priority during his term in office. Buxton's project was to establish a Canadian curling hall of fame.

Since at least the early 1950s, curling observers and executives periodically had raised the possibility of establishing a hall of fame. Buxton was the first to put a lot of time and effort into developing a concrete proposal. He headed an MCA group that presented an idea to the annual meeting of the CCA in 1972. The delegates to that meeting agreed in principle to forming a hall of fame in Winnipeg. Buxton was appointed chairman of an action committee to begin work on the project.[1]

From 1972 to 1981, Buxton explored the possibilities of using different sites. He was assisted by fellow-Winnipeggers Bert Cameron, "Charlie" Scrymgeour and, of course, Bob Picken and Cec Watt, two men whose energy and enthusiasm for curling projects were legendary by this time. A number of locations for the Hall were considered: the Winnipeg Stadium–Arena complex, the University of Manitoba, the Pan-Am Pool and Grant Park Shopping Centre, and the Convention Centre. All were rejected for one reason or another.[2]

Attention then shifted to the Assiniboine Park Pavilion, and in October 1983 a lease was signed with the City of Winnipeg to rent it. The Hall of Fame had until 1988 to raise the $1.5 million required to renovate the structure. Buxton and his supporters were already raising funds, and for the next two years they did so in earnest. Two primary sources of revenue were casinos and the Silver Broom Foundation. During this time plans were made also to hire an executive director, and office space was rented.

However, at the 1985 annual meeting of the CCA, a majority of delegates voted not to proceed with the establishment of a hall of fame. That is, they decided to keep inducting people into the Hall of Fame, as they had been since 1973, but not to establish and maintain a building for it. They were afraid of the expenses that administering a building might entail. They also felt a mobile hall would be more accessible to the majority of Canadian curlers. Accordingly, they arranged simply for a travelling exhibit of curling artifacts and memorabilia to be featured in particular at the Labatt Brier and Scott Tournament of Hearts, the annual national championship events for men and women, respectively.[3]

Their project halted, the Manitoba group decided to inaugurate a provincial hall of fame. The MCA and MLCA jointly took steps to establish a company, the Manitoba Curling Hall of Fame and Museum, Incorporated, which became a reality in the summer of 1987. Noel Buxton's ill health would not permit him to head the company;

143

Noel Buxton

he died late the next year. The president was Bob Picken and the secretary-treasurer was Bert Cameron, son of the founder of the Brier and himself a director of that event from 1965 to 1979. The new company successfully applied to the CCA for the return of funds raised in Manitoba for the Canadian Curling Hall of Fame. On December 6, 1987, exactly ninety-nine years after the MCA had been formed, the first inductees into the provincial Hall of Fame were recognized at a formal banquet. A search for a suitable site for the Manitoba Hall was already in progress.[4]

One hopes that the new provincial Curling Hall of Fame, the first in Canada, will be located at a site to which both curlers and non-curlers will be attracted. One hopes also that the provincial Hall of Fame will contain the items the national one should have possessed. That is, it should contain not only a list of names. It ought also to have a library with as many books, photographs, films and taped interviews as possible. It ought to have old rocks, brooms, sweaters, shoes, tam o'shanters, pins, whisky flasks and other objects associated with the sport. The directors of the hall should be able to take advantage of the fact that curlers generally have a keener sense of history than most althletes do, and they have items piled up in attics, garages, even outhouses that they would agree to make available to the general public.

Through its artifacts and displays, the provincial Curling Hall of Fame will depict many stories. One of these is the leading role Winnipeggers have played in the evolution of curling. In every era for a hundred years, the city has produced a large proportion of the world's top players. These athletes consistently have introduced or mastered new techniques or strategies. Winnipeggers have helped establish important national and international championship events. They also have hosted successfully a number of these events, and done so partly because members of the Winnipeg media have been more enthusiastic about curling than members of the media in other cities have been. Individuals from Winnipeg have taught men and women across the country and around the world how to curl competitively. Finally, Winnipeg has been the headquarters of a provincial curling association that consistently has arranged and administered the world's largest annual bonspiel.

If the Manitoba Curling Hall of Fame is able to illustrate these and other facts imaginatively, it will itself become one more reason for the world to regard Winnipeg as curling's capital.

Notes

INTRODUCTION

1. Rev. John Kerr, *Curling in Canada and the United States, A Record of the Tour of the Scottish Team, 1902-03, and of the Games in the Dominion and the Republic* (Toronto: Georgie A. Morton, 1904), pp. 452-454, 468.

2. Ibid., chapters 11 and 12, passim.

3. *Winnipeg Tribune* (hereafter *Trib.*), February 17, 1893, p. 5; *32nd Annual of the Ontario Curling Association* (1907), pp. 15-16; *Calgary Herald*, March 4, 1961, p. 2; Martin O'Malley, "The Life of Riley," *Saturday Night*, November 1984, p. 61; *Manitoba Free Press* (hereafter *FP*), February 15, 1907, p. 10, January 29, 1921, p. 19, April 19, 1923, p. 11, February 4, 1924, p. 16, February 2, 1927, p. 13, February 8, 1936, p. 23, February 12, 1938, p. 32, February 8, 1941, p. 21.

4. See J.H. Hexter on the Reality Rule and the Maximum Impact Rule in *The History Primer* (New York: Basic Books, Inc., 1971) especially p. 230.

5. See W.A. Creelman, *Curling Past and Present* (Toronto: McClelland and Stewart Ltd., 1950); W.H. Murray, *The Curling Companion*, revised edition (Don Mills, Ontario: Collin's Publishers, 1982); David B. Smith, *Curling: An Illustrated History* (Edinburgh: John Donald Publishers Ltd., 1981); Gerald Redmond, *The Sporting Scots of Nineteenth-Century Canada* (East Brunswick, N.J.: Associated University Presses, Inc., 1982), chapters 2 and 4; Robert Wayne Simpson, "The Influences of the Montreal Curling club on the Developmment of Curling in Canada, 1807-1857" (M.A. thesis, University of Western Ontario, 1980); E.C. Guillet, *Early Life in Upper Canada* (Toronto: The Ontario Publishing Co. Ltd., 1933), chapter 11; John A. Stevenson, *Curling in Ontario, 1846-1946* (Toronto: Ontario Curling Association, 1950).

6. For example, there is no entry under "curling" in the index to Alan Artibise's *Winnipeg: An Illustrated History* (Toronto: James Lorimer and Company and National Museums of Canada, 1977). But see Paul Voisey, *Vulcan: The Making of a Prairie Community* (Toronto: University of Toronto Press, 1988), pp. 163-165.

7. See Doug Maxwell and Friends, *The First Fifty: A Nostalgic Look at the Brier* (Toronto: Douglas D. Maxwell Ltd., 1980). See also the stimulating observations on curling by Max Braithwaite in *The Night We Stole the Mountie's Car* (Toronto: McClelland and Stewart Ltd., 1971), chapter 9.

8. Marshall McLuhan, "Games: The Extensions of Man," in *Understanding Media: The Extensions of Man* (Toronto: Signet Books, 1964), pp. 214-215.

CHAPTER 1

1. Creelman, *Curling Past and Present*, chapters 1-5; Murray, *Curling Companion*, chapters 1-4; Smith, *Illustrated History*, chapters 1-3, 10.

2. On curling in British North America, see Creelman, *Curling Past and Present*, pp. 127-141, passim.; Murray, *Curling Companion*, pp. 115-118; Smith, *Illustrated History*, pp. 130-135; Guillet, *Early Life in Upper Canada*, chapter 11; Stevenson, *Curling in Ontario*, passim.; Ian F. Jobling, "Sport in Nineteenth Century Canada: The Effects of Technological Change on its Development" (Ph.D. dissertation, University of Alberta, 1970), pp. 230-233; Simpson, "The Influences of the Montreal Curling Club."

3. *Annual of the Manitoba Branch, Royal Caledonian Curling Club* (hereafter *Annual, Manitoba Branch*), 9 (1897-98), p. 162.

4. Local legend holds that the Red River Scots curled often. See the welcoming messages of Premiers Duff Roblin, Ed Schreyer, Sterling Lyon and Howard Pawley, respectively, in the Manitoba Curling Association (hereafter MCA) *74th Annual Programme* (1962), p. 10, *83rd Annual Bonspiel Programme* (1971), p. 11, *92nd Annual Bonspiel Yearbook* (1980), p. 9, *94th Annual*

Bonspiel Yearbook (1982), p. 9. One would think there would be more references to the sport in the primary sources if men curled as often in the Settlement as legend suggests.

5. Nor'Wester, March 28, 1860, p. 4.

6. See the comments on Mr. I. W. Thompson of Portage la Prairie, in MCA 40th Annual Bonspiel Programme (1928), p. 17; see also FP, November 23, 1877, p. 1, February 12, 1938, p. 21.

7. FP, February 28, 1874, p. 1, March 14, 1874, p. 4, October 27, 1876, p. 3, November 9, 1876, p. 3, December 12, 1876, p. 3; Weekly FP, January 9, 1875, p. 4; Alexander Begg and Walter R. Nursey, Ten Years in Winnipeg: A Narration of the Principal Events in the History of the City of Winnipeg from the Year A.D. 1870 to the Year A.D. 1879, Inclusive (Winnipeg: Begg and Nursey, 1879), pp. 140, 142, 179; Granite Stone, "Winnipeg's Big 'Spiel," Western Sportsman, II (February 1906), p. 54; MCA 100th Annual Bonspiel Yearbook (1988), pp. 47, 67; Edward R.R. Mills, The Story of Stony Mountain and District (Winnipeg: Edward R.R. Mills, 1960), pp. 51, 53.

8. Kerr, Curling in Canada and the United States, chapters 11 and 12, passim.; FP, February 17, 1893, p. 5, February 15, 1894, p. 1 of special Bonspiel edition, February 5, 1898, p. 5.

9. FP, October 28, 1881, p. 1, November 1, 1881, p. 1, November 17, 1883, p. 4, November 19, 1883, p. 4; n.a., "Granite Curling Club – 1880-1955," in MCA 68th Annual Bonspiel Programme (1956), p. 27.

10. See MCA 56th Annual Bonspiel Programme (1944), p. 70.

11. FP, October 13, 1887, p.1, October 27, 1887, p. 1, November 3, 1887, p. 4, November 16, 1887, p. 1, November 21, 1887, p. 4; "History of the Thistle Curling Club," MCA 68th Annual Bonspiel Programme (1956), p. 33.

12. FP, December 4, 1882, p. 3, January 31, 1883, p. 8; Brandon Mail, November 2, 1883, p. 8; Margaret Morton Fahrni and W.L. Morton, Third Crossing: A History of the First Quarter Century of the Town and District of Gladstone in the Province of Manitoba (Winnipeg: W.L. Morton, 1946), p. 81; Smith, Illustrated History, pp. 139, 141.

13. Treherne Area History Committee, Tiger Hills to the Assiniboine (Treherne: Treherne Area History Committee, 1976), p. 90; n.a., Banner Country, History of Russell and District, 1879-1967 (Russell, Manitoba: Russell Women's Institute and Russell Chamber of Commerce,

1967), p. 43; n.a., Bridging the Years . . . Shoal Lake and District (Shoal Lake, Manitoba: Shoal Lake Anniversary Committee, 1959), p. 57; A.F. (Dick) McKenzie, The Lansdowne Story, Grain, Gravel, Growth (n.p.: Lansdowne Centennial Committee, 1967), p. 16; John E. Reid, "Sports and Games in Alberta Before 1900," (M.A. thesis, University of Alberta, 1969), p. 65.

14. W.L. Morton, Manitoba: A History, second edition (Toronto: University of Toronto Press, 1967), chapters 7-10; Morton, "A Century of Plain and Parkland," in Richard Allen (ed.), A Region of the Mind, Interpreting the Western Canadian Plains (Regina: Canadian Plains Research Center, 1973), pp. 168-171; Lewis G. Thomas, "Introduction," in Thomas (ed.), The Prairie West to 1905, A Canadian Sourcebook (Toronto: Oxford University Press, 1975), pp. 7, 13-14; J.E. Rea, "The Roots of Prairie Society," in David P. Gagan (ed.), Prairie Perspectives (Montreal and Toronto: Holt, Rinehart and Winston of Canada Ltd., 1970), especially pp. 46-50; Census of Manitoba, 1885-86, pp. 14-15, 22-23, 30-31.

15. Dennis Brailsford, Sport and Society, Elizabeth to Anne (Toronto: University of Toronto Press, 1969), chapter 4, especially p. 126; Goldwin French, "The Evangelical Creed in Canada," in Morton (ed.), The Shield of Achilles (Toronto: McClelland and Stewart Ltd., 1968), pp. 16-21; Robert W. Malcolmson, Popular Recreations in English Society, 1700-1850 (London: Cambridge University Press, 1973), pp. 105-107; E.P. Thompson, "Time, Work-Discipline and Industrial Capitalism," in M.W. Flinn and T.C. Smart (eds.), Essays in Social History (London: Oxford University Press, 1974), p. 63.

16. See especially Samuel Smiles, Self-Help, with Illustrations of Character and Conduct (Boston: Ticknor and Fields, 1861). See also FP, June 8, 1875, p. 3, and the following articles in the Journal of Education for Upper Canada: "To Young Men" (January 1848), p. 32; "The Importance of Resolution" (February 1848), p. 64; "The Reward of Diligence" 6 (January 1853), p. 13; "The Young Man's Leisure" 6 (January 1853), p. 28.

17. Malcolmson, Popular Recreations, p. 102.

18. Ibid., p. 103; Peter Bailey, Leisure and Class in Victorian England: Rational Recreation and the Contest for Control, 1830-1885 (Toronto: University of Toronto Press, 1978), pp. 67, 71; B.H. Harrison, "Work and Leisure in Industrial Society," Past and Present, no. 3 (April 1965), p. 101; Nor'Wester, March 31, 1864.

19. FP, April 18, 1877, p. 3, February 8, 1881, p. 1; Public Archives of Manitoba (hereafter PAM), Gerald Panting Collection, "Regional History Survey: Questionnaires and Interviews with Early Settlers of Southern Manitoba, 1953," interview with and questionnaire answered by J.A.F. Hill of Manitou, p. 4; Nellie McClung, Clearing in

the *West, My Own Story* (Toronto: Thomas Allen Ltd., 1935), p. 110.

20. *FP*, February 17, 1883, p. 8; February 17, 1894, p. 1; February 14, 1896, p. 1; February 8, 1897, p. 5; February 12, 1897, p. 4; *Trib.*, February 17, 1893, p. 5; James Hedley, "Curling in Canada," part II, *The Dominion Illustrated Monthly* (April 1892), p. 182.

21. When Manitobans spoke of "Anglo-Saxons" they had no genetically distinct race in mind. The term was used as a "synonym for a total culture" as Carl Berger says. That culture was understood to be the product of history and environment as well as of genes, and it was most certainly seen as shared by many Celts. See Carl Berger, *The Sense of Power: Studies in the Ideas of Canadian Imperialism, 1867-1914* (Toronto: University of Toronto Press, 1970), p. 117; *Trib.*, February 17, 1893, p. 5; n.a., "Weather and Climate," *The Western World*, 1 (March 1890), p. 10; James Fleming, "Report of YMCA Convention at Lake Geneva," *Manitoba College Journal*, 8 (November 1892, pp. 17-19).

22. See Doug Owram, *Promise of Eden: The Canadian Expansionist Movement and the Idea of the West, 1856-1900* (Toronto: University of Toronto Press, 1980), chapters 5 and 6; Carl Berger, "The True North Strong and Free," in J.M. Bumsted (ed.), *Interpreting Canada's Past*, vol. II: *After Confederation* (Toronto: Oxford University Press, pp. 158-170); Morris Mott, "The British-Protestant Pioneers and the Establishment of Manly Sports in Manitoba, 1870-1886," *Journal of Sport History*, 7 (Winter 1980), especially pp. 29-30; *FP*, February 7, 1880, p. 1, February 17, 1883, p. 8, October 22, 1887, p. 4, February 17, 1894, p. 1; F.B.B., "Winter Pastimes in Manitoba," *Canadian Magazine*, 10 (1898), p. 286; n.a., "Weather and Climate," p. 10.

23. Louis B. Wright, *Culture on the Moving Frontier* (New York: Harper and Brothers, 1961), pp. 20-21; Wright, *Life on the American Frontier* (New York: Capricorn Books, 1971), especially p. 235; Michael S. Cross, "The Age of Gentility: The Formation of an Aristocracy in the Ottawa Valley," in J.K. Johnson (ed.), *Historical Essays on Upper Canada* (Toronto: McClelland and Stewart Ltd., 1975), especially p. 227; Thomas, "Introduction," *The Prairie West*, especially p. 1.

24. Provincial Library of Manitoba (hereafter PLM), "Manitoba Biographies," B1, pp. 49-51; Mott, "Manly Sports and Manitobans: Settlement Days to World War One," (Ph.D. dissertation, Queen's University, 1980), pp. 85-86; Begg and Nursey, *Ten Years in Winnipeg*, p. 142; *FP*, December 12, 1876, p. 3, November 7, 1878, p. 1, November 1, 1881, p. 1; Manitoba Library Association, *Pioneers and Early Citizens of Manitoba: A Dictionary of Manitoba Biography from the Earliest Times to 1920* (Winnipeg: Peguis Publishers, 1971), pp. 10-11.

25. PLM, "Manitoba Biographies," B1, p. 41; Mott, "Manly Sports and Manitobans," p. 83; *FP*, November 7, 1878, p. 1, October 28, 1881, p. 1.

26. Begg and Nursey, *Ten Years in Winnipeg*, pp. 140, 142; *FP*, November 9, 1876, p. 3, December 12, 1876, p. 3, November 1, 1880, p. 1, October 28, 1881, p. 1, November 16, 1887, p. 1, April 13, 1922, p. 14, April 15, 1922, p. 9.

27. PLM, "Manitoba Biographies," B1, p. 78; "Winipeg Elite Files" in possession of Dr. G.A. Friesen, University of Manitoba, file on W.N. Kennedy; Mott, "Manly Sports and Manitobans," p. 84; Begg and Nursey, *Ten Years in Winnipeg*, p. 140; *FP*, November 9, 1876, p. 3, November 1, 1881, p. 1; *Winnipeg Times*, November 3, 1879, p. 4.

28. Manitoba Library Association, *Pioneers and Early Citizens*, pp. 14-15; Mills, *The Story of Stony Mountain and District*, pp. 62-64; *Henderson's Directories of Winnipeg, Manitoba and the Northwest* (1876-77 to 1887), especially the "miscellaneous" sections; *FP*, January 31, 1883, p. 8.

29. See *Brandon Daily Mail*, November 1, 1883, p. 8; *Brandon Sun*, January 17, 1884, p. 2, January 22, 1884, p. 2, February 19, 1885, p. 5; G.F. Barker, *Brandon: A City, 1881-1961* (Brandon: G.F. Barker, 1977), pp. 12, 22; Fahrni and Morton, *Third Crossing*, pp. 47, 81.

30. *FP*, February 17, 1883, p. 8, February 14, 1884, p. 4, February 16, 1884, p. 1, February 11, 1887, p. 4, February 12, 1887, p. 4, January 30, 1888, p. 4.

31. Ibid., February 17, 1883, p. 8, January 17, 1886, p. 4, October 14, 1886, p. 4, October 11, 1888, p. 1.

32. Ibid., October 11, 1888, p. 1, December 7, 1888, p. 1; *Annual, Manitoba Branch*, 1 (1889-1890), pp. 24-25.

33. Alan F.J. Artibise, *Winnipeg: A Social History of Urban Growth, 1874-1914* (Montreal and London: McGill-Queen's University Press, 1975), p. 130; Artibise (ed.), *Town and City: Aspects of Western Canadian Urban Development* (Regina: Canadian Plains Research Center, 1980), especially p. 430.

34. See *FP*, December 21, 1889, pp. 13, 16.

35. *Annual, Manitoba Branch*, 1 (1889-90), pp. 73-74, 6 (1894-95), pp. 26-27; *FP*, February 15, 1894, p. 1 of special Bonspiel edition; Redmond, *The Sporting Scots of Nineteenth Century Canada*, pp. 133, 155n.

36. *Annual, Manitoba Branch*, 15 (1903-04), p. 44; K.G. Jones, "Sport in Canada, 1900 to 1920" (Ph.D. dissertation, University of Alberta, 1970), pp. 246-250.

37. This outline of the format of bonspiels is drawn from press reports in the *FP* and the *Trib*.

38. *FP*, October 12, 1892, p. 5, November 21, 1892, p. 5, February 7, 1903, p. 18. A couple of other clubs had a very temporary existence in the 1880s or 1890s.

39. *FP*, October 22, 1892, p. 5, December 8, 1892, p. 5, December 13, 1892, p. 5, February 13, 1893, p. 5; *Trib.*, September 27, 1892, p. 5.

40. *Annual, Manitoba Branch*, 11 (1899-1900), p. 181. See also *FP*, February 12, 1892, p. 5, February 14, 1896, p. 1, February 11, 1898, p. 1.

41. On Pedley, see PLM, "Manitoba Biographies," B7, p. 204. Lists of officers of the Manitoba Branch and of all member clubs are given in each *Annual, Manitoba Branch*.

42. *FP*, February 12, 1894, p. 4.

43. Ibid., February 7, 1898, p. 1, February 19, 1900, p. 6.

44. Ibid., February 11, 1895, pp. 1, 4.

45. On chance as a factor in curling and in life, see reports of sermons in ibid., February 6, 1899, pp. 7, 5, February 14, 1916, p. 5.

46. Ibid., February 6, 1891, p. 5, February 16, 1894, p. 5, February 12, 1896, p. 1.

47. Smith, *Illustrated History*, chapter 12; Murray, *Curling Companion*, chapter 5.

48. MCA *88th Annual Bonspiel Yearbook* (1976), p. 43.

49. *FP*, December 29, 1898, p. 5, February 4, 1899, p. 8.

50. Ibid., December 26, 1892, p. 5, January 23, 1895, p. 6, February 4, 1899, p. 8; *Annual, Manitoba Branch*, 10 (1898-99), pp. 23-24.

51. Kerr, *Curling in Canada and the United States*, p. 475.

52. *FP*, January 14, 1880, p. 1, February 12, 1880, p. 1, February 16, 1884, p. 1, February 10, 1887, p. 4, February 6, 1888, p. 1, February 16, 1889, p. 1, February 25, 1889, p. 4, March 1, 1890, pp. 2, 8, March 5, 1890, p. 6, February 12, 1938, p. 21.

53. Event winners over the years are listed in the *Annual Yearbooks* of the Manitoba Curling Association. "Points" was a game in which individual curlers competed by making four attempts at each of nine different shots. They could sweep their own rocks, but could receive assistance only from a person who held a broom as a target. Each shot was graded with a "0," a "1" or a "2," according to how well it was played. Therefore the maximum score was 72 points.

54. *FP*, February 7, 1891, p. 5, February 12, 1898, p. 1.

55. Allan E. Cox, "A History of Sports in Canada, 1868-1900" (Ph.D. dissertation, University of Alberta, 1969), p. 219; Smith, *Illustrated History*, pp. 66-70; Simpson, "The Influences of the Montreal Curling Club," pp. 104-105, 120.

56. Kerr, *Scottish Curlers in Canada and the United States*, pp. 517, 525, 530; Smith, *Illustrated History*, pp. 82-89; Murray, *Curling Companion*, pp. 82, 121-122.

57. Smith, *Illustrated History*, pp. 70-72; Murray, *Curling Companion*, p. 121.

58. Smith, *Illustrated History*, pp. 54-56.

59. Kerr, *Scottish Curlers in Canada and the United States*, pp. 525-526, 530, 549, 573.

60. Ibid., pp. 526, 530, 544, 576.

61. *Annual, Manitoba Branch*, 10 (1898-99), p. 38.

62. *FP*, May 13, 1884, p. 4, April 8, 1886, p. 4, January 19, 1887, p. 4, February 15, 1894, p. 1 of special Bonspiel edition, February 22, 1902, p. 6, February 7, 1903, p. 19, June 7, 1937, p. 16, June 8, 1937, p. 14; *Manitoba Sun*, supplement to New Year's Illustrated Edition, December 1886.

63. Ken Watson, *Ken Watson on Curling* (Toronto: Copp Clark Publishing Company, 1950), p. 45; Smith, *Illustrated History*, p. 89; *FP*, January 10, 1906, p. 6; *FP*, January 10, 1906, p. 6; *Trib.*, February 17, 1910, p. 7.

CHAPTER 2

1. *Annual, Manitoba Branch*, 14 (1902-03), pp. 71-143; *FP*, February 7, 1903, p. 25.

2. MCA *Annual*, 26 (1914-15), pp. 106-161; MCA *75th Anniversary Bonspiel Program* (1963), pp. 100-103; *FP*, November 19, 1904, p. 5, December 30, 1908, p. 7, September 8, 1909, p. 6, October 19, 1911, p. 7, December 1, 1911, p. 7.

3. MCA *75th Annual Bonspiel Program* (1963), pp. 104, 107.

4. MCA *Annual*, 29 (1917-18), pp. 111-115. These pages do not list the members of the Union-Terminals Club. There must have been approximately 100 members in this club, going by the numbers from previous years.

5. MCA *75th Annual Bonspiel Program* (1963), pp. 108-110, 116, *33rd Annual Bonspiel Programme* (1920-21), pp. 44-45, *34th Annual Bonspiel Programme* (1922), pp. 11-13, *36th Annual Bonspiel Programme* (1924), pp. 6-8, *40th Annual Bonspiel Programme* (1928), pp. 6-8; *FP*, November 5, 1927, p. 34, November 7, 1927, p. 18, November 17, 1927, p. 20, November 19, 1927, p. 30, November 3, 1928, p. 32, November 16, 1928, p. 22.

6. *FP*, February 4, 1933, p. 23, December 29, 1913, p. 7, November 7, 1927, p. 18, MCA *100th Annual Bonspiel Programme* (1988), p. 77.

7. This figure is based on the assumption that between the end of the war and the end of the 1920s the growth in members of city clubs was in proportion to the growth in members of all MCA clubs.

8. *Winnipeg Saturday Post*, November 22, 1913, pp. 4-5; *FP*, January 31, 1914, p. 17.

9. *FP*, November 30, 1904, p. 5, November 22, 1913, p. 1 of sports section, January 6, 1914, p. 6, January 27, 1914, p. 6, January 17, 1916, p. 2, January 20, 1916, p. 6, January 28, 1916, p. 6, January 31, 1916, p. 6, March 9, 1916, p. 10, March 16, 1916, p. 6, February 4, 1920, p. 13, February 1, 1921, p. 17, February 2, 1921, p. 13, February 3, 1921, p. 17, February 20, 1922, p. 11, February 19, 1924, p. 18, February 20, 1924, p. 18, October 30, 1924, p. 18, December 27, 1924, p. 15.

10. Ibid., December 1, 1911, p. 7, December 3, 1912, p. 6, December 27, 1912, p. 6, September 20, 1913, p. 19; MCA *Annual*, 25 (1913-14), advertisement for Hingston Smith Arms Company in front section.

11. *Labour Gazette*, November 1912, p. 540, September 1913, p. 319, November 1913, p. 579.

12. These figures were generated by taking the membership lists from the relevant *Annuals* of the Manitoba Branch or MCA, and locating the names in *Henderson's Winnipeg Directories* for each year.

13. *FP*, February 15, 1894, p. 2 of special Bonspiel edition, February 14, 1896, p. 1, January 21, 1909, p. 6, February 12, 1912, p. 7.

14. See the reasons that the Grand Trunk Pacific Athletic Association was organized in 1913, outlined in *Winnipeg Saturday Post*, July 18, 1914, p. 5.

15. See Professor Joliffe, "On Sport," *Vox Wesleyana*, 13 (November 1908), pp. 25-26; *Winnipeg Voice*, September 8, 1911, p. 7, September 5, 1913, pp. 1-2. On this theme, see Joe Macguire, "Images of Manliness and Competing Ways of Living in Late Victorian and Edwardian Britain," *The British Journal of Sports History*, 3 (December 1986), pp. 265-287.

16. *FP*, July 11, 1889, p. 3; *Northwestern Sportsman*, April 8, 1896, p. 10; Ellen W. Gerber, Jan Felshin, Pearl Berlin and Waneen Wyrick, *The American Woman in Sport* (Reading, Mass.: Addision-Wesley Publishing Company, 1974), pp. 4, 9-17; Carroll Smith-Rosenberg and Charles Rosenberg, "The Female Animal: Medical and Biological Views of Woman and Her Role in Nineteenth Century America," *Journal of American History*, 60 (September 1973), pp. 332-338; Heather Rielly, "Attitudes to Women in Sport in Eastern Ontario – the Early Years 1867-1885," in *Proceedings, 5th Canadian Symposium on the History of Sport and Physical Education* (Toronto: University of Toronto School of Physical and Health Education, 1982), pp. 380-384; Helen Lenskyj, "Moral Physiology in Physical Education and Sport for Girls in Ontario, 1890-1930," in ibid., pp. 139-141.

17. The population of Winnipeg at various points is given in Artibise, *Winnipeg: An Illustrated History*, p. 202.

18. *Vox Wesleyana*, 12 (March 1908), p. 107; Geoffrey Harphan, "Time Running Out: The Edwardian Sense of Cultural Degeneration," *Clio*, 5 (Spring 1976), pp. 283-286; Stephanie Lee Twin, "Jock and Jill, Aspects of Women's Sports History in America, 1870-1940," (Ph.D. dissertation, Rutgers University, 1978), pp. 115-127; Anna Davin, "Imperialism and Motherhood," *History Workshop Journal*, 5 (Spring 1978), pp. 9-22.

19. H.R. Hadcock, "Physical Training," *Western School Journal*, 2 (April 1907), p. 106; *Vox Wesleyana*, 6 (July 1902), p. 153; *Dauphin Press*, October 28, 1909, p. 6; *Winnipeg Telegram*, April 12, 1913, sec. 3, p. 2; Lenskyj, "Femininity First, Sport and Physical Education for Ontario Girls, 1890-1930," *Canadian Journal of History of Sport*, 12 (December 1982), pp. 4-14; Smith-Rosenberg and Rosenberg, "The Female Animal," pp. 338-342.

20. M. Ann Hall, "A History of Women's Sport in Canada Prior to World War I" (Ph.D. dissertation, University of Alberta, 1966), pp. 102, 150; Allan E. Cox, "A History of Sports in Canada, 1868-1900" (Ph.D. dissertation, University of Alberta, 1969), pp. 384-385; Smith, *Illustrated History*, pp. 158-162; *Trib.*, October 29, 1908, p. 6.

21. *FP*, March 10, 1908, p. 6, March 11, 1908, p. 6, March 14, 1908, p. 11, March 16, 1908, p. 6.

22. Ibid., November 5, 1908, p. 6.

23. MCA *Annual*, 25 (1913-14), p. 160; *Winnipeg Saturday Post*, March 14, 1914, p. 5; Marion W. Abra (ed.), *A View of the Birdtail, A History of the Town of Birtle and the Villages of Foxwarren and Solsgirth, 1878-1974* (Birtle,

Man.: History Committee of the Municipality of Birtle, 1974), p. 198; n.a., *Our Story to 1970* (n.p.: Rural Municipality of Strathclair, 1970), p. 163.

24. MCA *Annual*, 25 (1913-14), p. 160; *FP*, February 4, 1926, p. 14; MCA *50th Annual Bonspiel Programme* (1938), p. 68.

25. *FP*, February 3, 1926, p. 16, February 9, 1914, p. 6, November 21, 1918, p. 13.

26. Ibid., December 30, 1908, p. 7, September 8, 1909, p. 6, February 9, 1914, p. 6, February 3, 1926, p. 16.

27. Ibid., February 3, 1926, p. 16; MCA *100th Annual Bonspiel Yearbook* (1988), p. 76.

28. *FP*, February 3, 1926, p. 16, December 7, 1909, p. 6, December 1, 1911, p. 7, December 14, 1912, p. 23, November 21, 1918, p. 13, February 7, 1928, pp. 1, 31, November 3, 1928, p. 32, November 16, 1928, p. 22, February 7, 1933, pp. 1, 6.

29. Ibid., February 3, 1926, p. 16; MCA *100th Annual Bonspiel Yearbook* (1988), pp. 74, 78, 93, 94, *75th Annual Bonspiel Programme* (1963), pp. 109, 116.

30. *FP*, December 14, 1912, p. 23; MCA *68th Annual Bonspiel Programme* (1956), p. 33, *100th Annual Bonspiel Yearbook* (1988), p. 68.

31. *FP*, December 14, 1912, p. 23, September 20, 1913, p. 19, January 9, 1914, p. 6; *Granite Curling Club's 75th Anniversary Pamphlet, 1880-1955* (copy in possession of M. Mott), p. 6; Sheila Grover, "The Granite Curling Club, 22 Mostyn Place, Winnipeg," *Manitoba History*, no. 14 (Autumn 1987), pp. 15-16; MCA *75th Annual Bonspiel Programme* (1963), p. 108.

32. *FP*, October 1, 1892, p. 5, December 8, 1892, p. 5, September 8, 1909, p. 6, December 7, 1909, p. 6, October 19, 1911, p, 7, December 1, 1911, p. 7, December 12, 1911, p. 6; interviews with Bob Picken, Winnipeg, May 2, 1989, C.H. Scrymgeour, Winnipeg, May 3, 1989.

33. *FP*, April 19, 1923, p. 11, February 15, 1907, p. 10, December 14, 1912, p. 23, January 29, 1921, p. 19.

34. See Ruben Bellan, *Winnipeg's First Century: An Economic History* (Winnipeg: Queenston House Publishing, 1978), especially chapters 7-10; and Paul Phillips, "The Prairie Urban System 1911-1961: Specialization and Change," in Artibise (ed.), *Town and City*, especially pp. 11-22.

35. *FP*, November 29, 1905, p. 6, April 18, 1918, p. 6, April 19, 1928, p. 20.

36. See Bil Gilbert, "Pitchin' Shoes," *Sports Illustrated*, September 24, 1984, especially pp. 69-74; Voisey, *Vulcan*, especially pp. 163-165.

37. *FP*, January 8, 1914, p. 6, February 4, 1914, p. 6, February 2, 1921, p. 13.

38. Stevenson, *Curling in Ontario, 1846-1946*, p. 237; Cecil R. Blackburn, "The Development of Sports in Alberta, 1900-1918," (M.A. thesis, University of Alberta, 1974), pp. 183-184; Saskatchewan Curling Association, *Programme of the 25th Annual Bonspiel* (1929), p. 3; *Saskatchewan Curling Association Yearbook* (1931-32), p. 29.

39. Lists of officers can be found near the front of every MCA *Annual* or *Bonspiel Programme*.

40. *FP*, July 30, 1920, pp. 1, 15, August 3, 1920, p. 8, August 4, 1920, p. 10; *Trib.*, January 18, 1909, p. 6; *Regina Morning Leader*, January 14, 1908, p. 1, January 20, 1908, p. 5, January 21, 1908, p. 5.

41. On O'Grady, see *FP*, November 4, 1914, p. 12; PLM, *Manitoba Biographies*, B2, p. 135. On the O'Grady Trophy, see Bruce Boreham, "The O'Grady Challenge Cup," MCA *59th Annual Bonspiel Programme* (1947), pp. 26-27. Some information here comes also from *FP*, February 3, 1911, p. 6, and from an interview with Howard Wood, Sr., November 29, 1976.

42. *FP*, September 7, 1936, p. 6, February 8, 1916, p. 6, February 11, 1922, p. 24; MCA *38th Annual Bonspiel Programme* (1926), pp. 55-57; *Saskatchewan Curling Association Yearbook* (1932-33), p. 31; *Regina Leader-Post*, January 9, 1930, p. 15.

43. MCA *50th Annual Bonspiel Programme* (1938), unpaginated front section; *FP*, April 18, 1918, p. 6.

44. PLM, *Manitoba Biographies*, B6, p. 218, B7, p. 235; *FP*, April 12, 1919, pp. 1, 4; George Bryce, *The Scotsman in Canada*, vol. II, *Western Canada* (Toronto: The Musson Book Company, Ltd., 1911), pp. 333-334.

45. MCA *50th Annual Bonspiel Programme* (1938), pp. 33-34, 69-70; *FP*, November 9, 1916, p. 10.

46. MCA *98th* [actually 97th] *Annual Bonspiel Yearbook* (1985), p. 35.

47. *FP*, February 11, 1922, p. 24, February 11, 1924, p. 16, February 5, 1926, p. 16, February 9, 1926, p. 16. At one bonspiel in the 1920s a men's rink from Arden showed up with a woman on it. This created more interest than controversy, but, before the next bonspiel, a regulation was passed which allowed women to curl only in the women's events. See *FP*, February 10, 1951, p. 18.

48. *FP*, February 13, 1890, p. 5, February 12, 1892, p. 5, December 12, 1896, p. 5, November 15, 1897, p. 5, January 7, 1898, p. 5, February 14, 1898, p. 3, October 24, 1904, p. 6; Jones, "Sport in Canada," p. 250; *Annual, Manitoba Branch*, 15 (1903-04), pp. 53-54; MCA *100th Anniversary Bonspiel Yearbook* (1988), p. 49.

49. The 1913 bonspiel, for example, had 180 rinks, and ninety-seven came from outside the city. In 1917, 120 of the 192 rinks entered were from non-Winnipeg clubs, in 1922, 141 of 250, and in 1927, 97 of 188.

50. The names of the curlers are listed in the *Annual, Manitoba Branch*, 17 (1905-06), pp. 123-129. These names were checked through *Henderson's North-West Gazetteer and Directory, 1905*. The assumption has been that individuals listed as barbers, blacksmiths and jewellers were independent businessmen.

51. The names of the curlers are provided in MCA *Annual*, 25 (1913-14), pp. 41-45. The occupations of these curlers have been checked by searching through the following local histories: History Book Committee of Neepawa, *Heritage: Neepawa Land of Plenty* (Neepawa: History Book Committee of Neepawa, Manitoba, 1983); Abra, *A View of the Birdtail*; Cartwright and District History Committee, *Memories Along the Badger Revisited: Cartwright and District, 1885-1985* (Cartwright: Cartwright and District History Committee, 1985); Jack Lamb, et al., *Newdale 1870-1970* (Newdale: Newdale Historical Society, 1970); Evelyn Mullin, *Living Gold: A History of the Rural Municipality of Roland, Manitoba, 1876-1976* (Roland: Myrtle-Roland History Book Committee, 1978); Rapid City and District Historical Society, *Rapid City and District: Our Past and Our Future* (Rapid City: Rapid City Historical Society, 1978); n.a., *Trails Along the Pipestone* (Pipestone: Rural Municipality of Pipestone, 1981).

52. Dennis Sparling, "The Oak River Men's Curling Club, 1900-1920" (unpublished term paper in possession of M. Mott, prepared for course 11:379 at the University of Manitoba, n.d.), pp. 5-7; *Souris Plaindealer*, October 18, 1907, p. 1; *Report on a Rural Survey of the Agricultural, Educational, Social and Religious Life, Turtle Mountain District, Manitoba, including the Municipalities of Whitewater, Morton and Winchester* (n.p.: Departments of Social Science and Evangelism of the Presbyterian and Methodist Churches, 1914), p. 28.

53. On the importance of being psychologically "ready" to appreciate humour, see Neil Schaeffer, *The Art of Laughter* (New York: Columbia University Press, 1981), especially pp. 17-18.

54. *FP*, February 18, 1918, p. 7. For the jokes and good humour at other functions see the reports in ibid., February 16, 1910, pp. 6, 10, February 14, 1911, p. 18, February 15, 1915, p. 6, February 14, 1916, p. 11, February 16, 1920, p. 11, February 21, 1921, pp. 1, 16, February 20, 1922, p. 20. For information on the reasons that people laugh and on the occasions on which they do, see especially Norman N. Holland, *Laughing: A Psychology of Humour* (Ithaca, New York: Cornell University Press, 1982), especially chapters 2, 9, 10 and 11.

55. *FP*, April 18, 1918, p. 6, April 22, 1920, p. 15, February 5, 1921, p. 16, November 17, 1921, p. 17, February 4, 1922, p. 16, April 20, 1922, p. 11.

56. Ibid., January 19, 1916, p. 1. See also MCA *Annual*, 23 (1911-12), p. 39; *Winnipeg Saturday Post*, February 18, 1911, p. 15.

57. *FP*, January 11, 1916, p. 8, January 19, 1916, p. 1, February 8, 1919, p. 16, February 4, 1922, p. 16.

58. Ibid., February 9, 1918, p. 29, February 9, 1892, p. 5, January 29, 1894, p. 5.

59. For lists of donors and for statements of revenue and expenses, see MCA *Annual*, 19 (1907-08), pp. 58-63; MCA *39th Annual Bonspiel Programme* (1927), pp. 57-61. See also *FP*, February 27, 1915, p. 3, March 4, 1916, p. 10.

60. MCA *98th* [actually 97th] *Annual Bonspiel Yearbook* (1985), p. 85.

61. Ibid., p. 39.

62. MCA *Annual*, 29 (1917-18), pp. 79, 83; *FP*, February 18, 1918, p. 6, February 17, 1919, pp. 1, 8, February 16, 1920, p. 1, February 14, 1921, p. 1; *Trib.*, February 12, 1923, p. 12.

63. *FP*, February 12, 1913, p. 7, February 6, 1917, p. 12, February 18, 1918, p. 7, January 29, 1921, p. 19; Jack Ludwig, "Rocks of all Ages," *Maclean's*, February 1974, p. 66.

64. *FP*, January 10, 1906, p. 6, February 12, 1938, p. 21, February 18, 1939, p. 25; February 25, 1939, p. 22, February 10, 1940, pp. 21, 22, February 19, 1941, p. 16; *Trib.*, February 5, 1910, p. 11, February 12, 1910, p.3, February 8, 1955, p. 20.

65. All of this is based on *Annuals* of the Manitoba Branch or MCA, 1903 to 1917, plus MCA *98th* [actually 97th] *Annual Bonspiel Yearbook* (1985), pp. 39-87; Watson, *Ken Watson on Curling*, p. 47; Smith, *Illustrated History*, p. 90; Murray, *Curling Companion*, p. 123; *FP*, February 24, 1914, p. 6, February 12, 1923, p. 13, February 18, 1939, p. 25, February 25, 1939, p. 22, March 3, 1952, p. 24, October 20, 1953, p. 18; *Trib.*, January 8, 1910, p. 9, February 9, 1955, p. 20.

66. Major M.H. Marshall, *The Scottish Curlers in Canada and U.S.A., 1922-23* (Edinburgh: Edinburgh University Press, 1924), p. 333. See also ibid., pp. 337-348, passim.; *FP*, February 10, 1920, p. 4.

67. MCA *Annual*, 21 (1909-10), p. 138, *Annual*, 22 (1910-11), p. 49, *98th* [actually 97th] *Bonspiel Yearbook* (1985), pp. 39-87; *FP*, February 8, 1924, p. 1, March 7, 1936, p. 1, March 2, 1946, p. 15, July 11, 1959, pp. 4, 49; *Trib.*, July 11, 1959, pp. 29, 37; interviews with C.H. Scrymgeour, Winnipeg, June 23, July 15, 1987, Lyle Dyker, Winnipeg, July 3, July 12, 1987, E. R. McKnight, Brandon, June 21, 1987, Russell Barker, Glenboro, January 13, 1987, Bruce Hudson, Winnipeg, July 15, 1987; Watson, *Ken Watson on Curling*, pp. 47-50; Vince Leah, "Immortal with a Broom," in Leah, *Pages from the Past* (Winnipeg: *Winnipeg Tribune*, 1975), pp. 50-52.

CHAPTER 3

1. *FP*, February 24, 1930, p. 6, March 16, 1949, p. 20.

2. The information that follows on Cameron is drawn from MCA *51st Annual Bonspiel Programme* (1939), p. 53, and *FP*, January 11, 1945, p. 1.

3. The story of the founding of the Brier can be found in Bruce Boreham, "How It All Began," in Maxwell and Friends, *The First Fifty*, pp. 32-33; Boreham, "The Story of 'The Brier,'" in Bruce Boreham (ed.), *The Story of "The Brier," Canada's Curling Classic . . . from A Humble Start in 1927 . . . Now Our Greatest Annual Amateur Sports Event* (n.p.; Bruce Boreham, 1970), no page numbers; Ernie Richardson, Joyce McKee and Doug Maxwell, *Curling: an authoritative handbook of techniques and strategy of the ancient game of curling* (Toronto: Thomas Allen Ltd., 1962), pp. 103-104. Important information has been obtained from *FP*, March 10, 1925, p. 14, March 6, 1940, p. 16; and MCA *38th Annual Bonspiel Programme* (1926), p. 19. On Walter F. Payne, see PLM, *Manitoba Biographies*, B12, p. 239, B9, p. 10. On John T. Haig, see MCA *49th Annual Bonspiel Programme* (1937), p. 55, and *FP*, October 25, 1962, p. 27. On Peter Lyall, see MCA *42nd Annual Bonspiel Programme* (1930), p. 57, and *FP*, May 7, 1945, p. 21.

4. *FP*, February 24, 1927, p. 17.

5. Boreham, "How It All Began," p. 33.

6. *FP*, February 26, 1929, p. 21.

7. Marshall, *Scottish Curlers in Canada and U.S.A.*, p. 218.

8. See *FP*, February 22, 1930, p. 32, February 27, 1932, p. 21, March 4, 1935, p. 14, March 2, 1936, p. 14, March 1, 1937, p. 15, February 28, 1938, p. 17.

9. Ibid., February 10, 1936, p. 12, April 22, 1937, p. 19, February 5, 1952, p. 16.

10. Ibid., February 12, 1917, p. 6, February 10, 1932, p. 1, February 13, 1935, pp. 1, 15, February 18, 1937, p. 16.

11. *Trib.*, March 2, 1940, p. 19.

12. Survey of the following papers in 1910: *Winnipeg Tribune, Manitoba Free Press, Winnipeg Telegram, Toronto World, Toronto Mail and Empire, Toronto Star, Toronto Telegram, Toronto Globe and Mail, Edmonton Bulletin, Edmonton Journal, Regina Leader-Post*; survey of the following papers in 1930: *Winnipeg Tribune, Manitoba Free Press, Toronto Mail and Empire, Toronto Telegram, Toronto Globe and Mail, Toronto Star, Edmonton Bulletin, Edmonton Journal, Regina Leader-Post.*

13. *FP*, March 2, 1970, p. 4 of special Brier section, January 24, 1987, p. 87; PLM, "Biographical Scrapbooks," B 16, p. 276; Barbara Huck, "Spectator Sports Persons," in Marjorie Earl (ed.), *Torch on the Prairies: A Portrait of Journalism in Manitoba 1859-1988* (Winnipeg: The Nor'Westers, 1988), pp. 81-82.

14. *FP*, February 9, 1955, pp. 6, 20; interview with Jack Matheson, Winnipeg, August 25, 1987; Huck, "Spectator Sports Persons," p. 82.

15. *FP*, March 7, 1958, p. 19, April 1, 1969, p. 34, March 27, 1978, p. 36; *Calgary Albertan*, March 6, 1961, "Welcome Curlers" section, no pages; interview with Jack Matheson, Winnipeg, August 25, 1987; Maxwell and Friends, *The First Fifty*, p. 114.

16. MCA *53rd Annual Bonspiel Programme* (1941), p. 10; *Edmonton Bulletin*, March 6, 1940, p. 12, March 8, 1940, p. 14; *Vancouver Sun*, March 8, 1940, p. 26; *FP*, March 8, 1940, pp. 16, 17, March 7, 1942, p. 21; MCA *75th Annual Bonspiel Programme* (1963), p. 58.

17. MCA *75th Annual Bonspiel Programme* (1963), pp. 51, 59; Boreham, *The Story of "The Brier*," "chapter 1940."

18. *Toronto Daily Star*, March 8, 1940, p. 15.

19. *FP*, March 3, 1942, p. 14, March 4, 1946, p. 13, March 22, 1948, p. 15; Bill Good, "When the Brier Went Big Time," in Maxwell and Friends, *The First Fifty*, pp. 44-46.

20. These statistics have been compiled from data in Richardson, McKee and Maxwell, *Curling*, pp. 109-118.

21. *FP*, March 8, 1940, p. 17, March 8, 1941, pp. 31, 33; Richardson, McKee and Maxwell, *Curling*, pp. 124-154.

22. *FP*, March 3, 1952, p. 31; Richardson, McKee and Maxwell, *Curling*, pp. 147-154.

23. *FP*, March 3, 1952, p. 31; Richardson, McKee and Maxwell, *Curling*, pp. 147-149.

24. Watson, *Ken Watson on Curling*, p. 162; *FP*, April 9, 1977, p. 45; Richardson, McKee and Maxwell, *Curling*, p. 149.

25. *FP*, March 8, 1946, p. 13, March 10, 1950, p. 20, March 1, 1954, p. 19.

26. Richardson, McKee and Maxwell, *Curling*, pp. 134-141; interview with Frank Avery, Vancouver, July 8, 1987.

27. *Vancouver Sun*, January 21, 1960, p. C3; *FP*, August 29, 1912, p. 7, January 22, 1960, p. 23; *Annuals*, Manitoba Branch, 16 (1904-05), p. 154, 18 (1906-07), p. 80; MCA *Annuals* 21 (1909-10), p. 52, 22 (1910-11), p. 52; MCA *98th* [actually 97th] *Annual Bonspiel Yearbook* (1985), p. 39; Richardson, McKee and Maxwell, *Curling*, pp. 135-139.

28. Doug Maxwell, "Beginning Years, 1927-1942," in Maxwell and Friends, *The First Fifty*, p. 8; interview with Frank Avery, Vancouver, July 8, 1987.

29. This is an argument advanced by Garnet Campbell. It makes sense. Interview with Garnet Campbell, Avonlea, Sask., January 5, 1988.

30. See comments by Leo Johnson in *FP*, March 14, 1934, p. 17, and March 2, 1946, p. 5, as well as those by Ken Watson in *Ken Watson on Curling*, pp. 132-133.

31. See *FP*, March 20, 1905, p. 5, February 18, 1922, p. 17, December 26, 1928, p. 13, December 31, 1947, p. 14.

32. Interviews with Ab Gowanlock, Dauphin, December 21, 1986, C.H. Scrymgeour, Winnipeg, June 23, 1987, Lyle Dyker, Winnipeg, July 3, 1987.

33. See the receptions given to Brier-winning teams reported in *FP*, March 12, 1947, p. 1, March 16, 1949, p. 20, March 13, 1956, p. 18.

34. Allan Fotheringham, "If these people must get their rocks off, can't they do it somewhere else?," *Maclean's*, April 3, 1978, p. 80.

35. See discussions on the definition of sport in Morris Mott, *Sports in Canada: Historical Readings* (Mississauga, Ont.: Copp Clark Pitman Ltd., 1989), p. 15; John W. Loy, Barry D. McPherson and Gerald Kenyon, *Sport and Social Systems: A Guide to the Analysis, Problems and Literature* (Reading, Mass.: Addison-Wesley

Publishing Company, 1978), pp. 3-10; Wilbert Marcellus Leonard II, *A Sociological Perspective of Sport* (Minneapolis, Minn.: Burgess Publishing Company, 1980), pp. 7-14.

36. *Trib.*, March 2, 1928, p. 15, March 3, 1928, p. 1, March 2, 1929, p. 22; *FP*, February 22, 1919, p. 12, February 8, 1923, p. 10, March 2, 1928, p. 15, March 3, 1928, p. 1, March 2, 1929, p. 33.

37. *FP*, March 4, 1925, p. 16, February 25, 1926, p. 15, March 3, 1926, p. 16.

38. MCA *43rd Annual Bonspiel Programme* (1931), p. 36; MCA *Annuals*, 23 (1911-12), p. 52, 24 (1912-13), p. 55, 25 (1913-14), pp. 44-45, 26 (1914-15), p. 49, 27 (1915-16), pp. 42-43, 28 (1916-17), p. 34; *FP*, March 1, 1930, p. 32, February 25, 1939, p. 22, March 8, 1940, p. 16, December 29, 1978, pp. 23, 41; *Trib.*, December 30, 1978, p. 29; *Edmonton Bulletin*, March 5, 1940, p. 12; interviews with Russell Barker, Glenboro, January 13, 1987, E.R. McKnight, Brandon, June 21, 1987, C.H. Scrymgeour, Winnipeg, June 23, 1987, Lyle Dyker, Winnipeg, July 12, 1987; Watson, *Ken Watson on Curling*, p. 91.

39. MCA *44th Annual Bonspiel Programme* (1932), p. 36, *53rd Annual Bonspiel Programme* (1941), p. 66, *98th* [actually 97th] *Annual Bonspiel Yearbook* (1985), pp. 39-87; *FP*, March 6, 1931, p. 1, March 2, 1946, p. 15, March 15, 1976, p. 35; *Trib.*, March 13, 1976, p. 45; interviews with Bruce Hudson, Winnipeg, July 15, 1987, Lyle Dyker, Winnipeg, July 3, July 12, 1987, C.H. Scrymgeour, Winnipeg, June 23, 1987.

40. MCA *43rd Annual Bonspiel Programme* (1931), p. 36, *45th Annual Bonspiel Programme* (1933), p. 36; MCA *Annuals*, 24 (1912-13), p. 55, 25 (1913-14), pp. 44-45, 26 (1914-15), p. 49; *FP*, February 25, 1932, p. 8, March 4, 1932, p. 1, February 18, 1939, p. 25, October 10, 1947, p. 27, October 11, 1947, p. 17.

41. MCA *98th* [actually 97th] *Annual Bonspiel Yearbook* (1985), pp. 39-87; *FP*, March 9, 1934, p. 1, March 2, 1946, p. 15, March 7, 1946, p. 15, March 8, 1946, p. 13, March 8, 1976, p. 11; *Trib.*, March 8, 1976, p. 25; interviews with Lyle Dyker, Winnipeg, July 12, 1987, C.H. Scrymgeour, Winnipeg, June 23, 1987, Bruce Hudson, Winnipeg, July 15, 1987, Andy McWilliams, Winnipeg, April 30, 1989; Jack Matheson, "The Brier Builds Character(s)," in Maxwell and Friends, *The First Fifty*, p. 69.

42. Watson, *Ken Watson on Curling*, passim; Maxwell, "Beginning Years, 1927-1942," in Maxwell and Friends, *The First Fifty*, pp. 4-8; Boreham, *The Story of "The Brier*," "chapter 1936," "chapter 1942," "chapter 1949"; MCA *88th Annual Bonspiel Yearbook* (1976), p. 9, *98th* [actually 97th] *Annual Bonspiel Yearbook* (1985), pp.

39-87; G. Redmond, "Watson, Ken," *The Canadian Encyclopedia*, vol. III (Edmonton: Hurtig Publishers, 1985), p. 1925; *Trib.*, March 11, 1949, p. 18; *FP*, March 3, 1936, p. 13, March 6, 1936, p. 16, March 6, 1942, p. 23, March 2, 1946, p. 15, March 8, 1949, p. 1, March 10, 1949, p. 18, March 11, 1949, p. 1, March 3, 1951, p. 18, March 5, 1952, p. 1, March 10, 1955, p. 20, July 30, 1986, pp. 46, 54; interviews with E.R. McKnight, Brandon, June 21, 1987, Russell Barker, Glenboro, June 13, 1987, C.H. Scrymgeour, Winnipeg, June 23, 1987, Lyle Dyker, Winnipeg, July 12, 1987, Jimmy Welsh, Winnipeg, July 3, 1987, Bruce Hudson, Winnipeg, July 15, 1987; MCA *49th Annual Bonspiel Programme* (1937), p. 16.

43. MCA *60th Annual Bonspiel Programme* (1948), pp. 77-78, *98th* [actually 97th] *Annual Bonspiel Yearbook* (1985), pp. 39-87; *FP*, February 20, 1937, p. 1, March 6, 1937, pp. 1, 27, February 26, 1942, p. 16, March 6, 1947, p. 1, March 7, 1947, p. 16, March 4, 1954, p. 23, March 6, 1954, p. 27; interviews with E.R. McKnight, Brandon, June 23, 1987, C. H. Scrymgeour, Winnipeg, June 23, July 15, 1987, Lyle Dyker, Winnipeg, July 12, 1987, Bruce Hudson, Winnipeg, July 15, 1987, Ab Gowanlock, Dauphin, December 21, 1986.

44. MCA *98th* [actually 97th] *Annual Bonspiel Yearbook* (1985), pp. 39-87; Boreham, *The Story of "The Brier*," "chapter 1952," "chapter 1956"; Larry McDorman, "The Greatest Shot in Brier History," *Atlantic Advocate*, 75 (February 1985), pp. 14-15; *FP*, March 3, 1952, p. 31, October 8, 1971, p. 45, October 9, 1971, p. 35; *Trib.*, October 8, 1971, pp. 15, 17; interviews with Lyle Dyker, Winnipeg, July 12, 1987, C.H. Scrymgeour, Winnipeg, June 23, July 15, 1987, Bruce Hudson, Winnipeg, July 15, 1987, Andy McWilliams, Winnipeg, April 30, 1989, Bob Picken, Winnipeg, May 2, 1989.

45. *Edmonton Journal*, March 21, 1970, p. 36; *FP*, March 4, 1950, p. 19, March 3, 1952, p. 25.

46. MCA *98th* [actually 97th] *Annual Bonspiel Yearbook* (1985), pp. 39-87, 51st *Annual Bonspiel Programme* (1939), p. 18; Scott Young, "Curling Town," *Maclean's*, February 15, 1942, pp. 16, 25-27; *FP*, February 15, 1935, p. 16, February 18, 1938, p. 16, March 4, 1938, p. 18, March 7, 1953, p. 1; *Brandon Sun*, September 30, 1988, p. 12; interviews with E.R. McKnight, Brandon, June 21, 1987, Ab Gowanlock, Dauphin, December 21, 1986, Jimmy Welsh, Winnipeg, July 3, 1987, Lyle Dyker, Winnipeg, July 3, July 12, 1987, C.H. Scrymgeour, Winnipeg, June 23, July 15, 1987, Bruce Hudson, Winnipeg, July 15, 1987, Russell Barker, Glenboro, January 13, 1987.

47. Watson, *Ken Watson on Curling*, p. 162; *FP*, April 9, 1977, p. 45; interviews with Lyle Dyker, Winnipeg, July 3, July 12, 1987, C.H. Scrymgeour, Winnipeg, June 23, July 15, 1987, Bruce Hudson, Winnipeg, July 15, 1987, E.R. McKnight, Brandon, June 21, 1987.

48. *FP*, February 21, 1947, p. 1; interviews with Jimmy Welsh, Winnipeg, July 3, 1987, Lyle Dyker, Winnipeg, July 12, 1987, C.H. Scrymgeour, Winnipeg, June 23, July 15, 1987, Bruce Hudson, Winnipeg, July 15, 1987.

49. Watson, *Ken Watson on Curling*, p. 163; interviews with E.R. McKnight, Brandon, June 21, 1987, C.H. Scrymgeour, Winnipeg, June 23, 1987, Lyle Dyker, Winnipeg, July 12, 1987, Ab Gowanlock, Dauphin, December 21, 1986, Russell Barker, Glenboro, January 13, 1987; *FP*, May 12, 1983, p. 44.

50. *FP*, February 15, 1940, p. 15, March 8, 1940, p. 22.

51. Ibid., March 10, 1952, p. 33; interviews with Lyle Dyker, Winnipeg, July 3, July 12, 1987, Bruce Hudson, Winnipeg, July 15, 1987.

52. *FP*, March 12, 1951, p. 21.

53. Watson, *Ken Watson on Curling*, pp. 157-160; interviews with Lyle Dyker, Winnipeg, July 3, July 12, 1987.

54. *FP*, March 2, 1946, p. 15; interviews with E.R. McKnight, Brandon, June 21, 1987, Russell Barker, Glenboro, January 13, 1987, C.H. Scrymgeour, Winnipeg, June 23, July 15, 1987, Lyle Dyker, Winnipeg, July 3, July 12, 1987, Bruce Hudson, Winnipeg, July 15, 1987.

55. *FP*, March 4, 1938, p. 18; interviews with C.H. Scrymgeour, Winnipeg, June 23, July 15, 1987, Lyle Dyker, Winnipeg, July 3, July 12, 1987; MCA *100th Annual Bonspiel Yearbook* (1988), p. 163.

56. MCA *100th Annual Bonspiel Yearbook* (1988), pp. 99, 163; *FP*, February 18, 1939, p. 25, February 25, 1939, p. 22; *Trib.*, February 14, 1923, p. 14; MCA *35th Annual Bonspiel Programme* (1923), pp. 24-25, 28-29, *36th Annual Bonspiel Programme* (1924), p. 33.

57. *FP*, February 26, 1942, p. 16, February 21, 1947, p. 1; interviews with C.H. Scrymgeour, Winnipeg, June 23, July 12, 1987, Lyle Dyker, Winnipeg, July 3, July 12, 1987, E.R. McKnight, Brandon, June 21, 1987, Bruce Hudson, Winnipeg, July 15, 1987, Jimmy Welsh, Winnipeg, July 3, 1987.

58. We have benefitted from conversations on this point in interviews with Lyle Dyker, Winnipeg, July 3, July 12, 1987, Terry Braunstein, Winnipeg, September 2, 1987, and Bryan Wood, Brandon, September 21, 1987.

59. *FP*, March 7, 1942, p. 21, March 8, 1950, p. 18, March 9, 1951, p. 20, March 6, 1954, p. 27.

60. Ibid., February 12, 1938, p. 32.

61. Ibid., April 19, 1928, p. 20, November 22, 1934, p. 19, April 16, 1936, p. 16, April 20, 1939, p. 16, April 20, 1944, p. 14, April 20, 1950, p. 20, April 29, 1955, p. 47, April 29, 1960, p. 51.

62. MCA 70th Annual Bonspiel Programme (1958), pp. 27-30, 98th [actually 97th] Annual Bonspiel Yearbook (1985), pp. 27-33.

63. MCA 75th Annual Bonspiel Programme (1963), pp. 105-106, 112-115, 100th Annual Bonspiel Yearbook (1988), pp. 70-73, 77, 83-84, 88, 91-92, 97; FP, November 21, 1913, p. 6.

64. FP, February 12, 1937, p. 19.

65. Ibid., November 22, 1946, p. 17, November 26, 1946, p. 13; interviews with Lyle Dyker, Winnipeg, July 3, 1987, and Jimmy Welsh, Winnipeg, July 3, 1987.

66. MCA 76th Annual Bonspiel Programme (1964), p. 30; FP, April 28, 1967, p. 46.

67. Artibise, Winnipeg: An Illustrated History, p. 207; Census of Canada, 1931, vol. 1, pp. 717-718, 793.

68. MCA 70th Annual Bonspiel Programme (1958), pp. 27-30; MCA 98th [actually 97th] Annual Bonspiel Yearbook (1985), pp. 27-33.

69. MCA 100th Annual Bonspiel Yearbook (1988), p. 83; FP, November 22, 1946, p. 17.

70. MCA 62nd Annual Bonspiel Programme (1950), p. 5, 68th Annual Bonspiel Programme (1956), p. 5, 69th Annual Bonspiel Programme (1957), p. 5; Elmwood Curling Club Minute Books, 1916-28, p. 177; Elmwood Curling Club Record Books, 1928-1938, pp. 230-231; Elmwood Curling Club Minute Books, 1942-1963, no pages, entry from 1950-51. Thanks to the Elmwood Curling Club and especially Gary McEwan for making the Elmwood documents available.

71. FP, February 12, 1895, p. 5, February 12, 1907, p. 10; January 7, 1955, p. 19; Fred W. Graham, "Baled Hay Rinks," Maclean's, December 15, 1938, p. 36; Peter Humeniuk, Hardships and Progress of Ukrainian Pioneers Memoirs from Stuartburn Colony and Other Points (Steinbach, Manitoba: Derksen Printers Ltd., 1977), p. 123; Leible Hershfield, The Jewish Athlete: A Nostalgic View (Winnipeg: Leible Hershfield, 1980), pp. 133-134; Paul Yuzyk, The Ukrainians in Manitoba: A Social History (Toronto: University of Toronto Press, 1953), pp. 156-157.

72. MCA 60th Anniversary Bonspiel Programme (1948), p. 85, 75th Anniversary Bonspiel Programme (1963), pp. 54-55; FP, April 27, 1962, p. 45.

73. FP, April 22, 1937, p. 19, March 14, 1944, p. 1.

74. MCA 75th Annual Bonspiel Programme (1963), pp. 56-57; FP, April 21, 1938, p. 18; interview with Bruce Hudson, Winnipeg, July 15, 1987; Trib., March 7, 1946, p. 13.

75. MCA 42nd Annual Bonspiel Programme (1930), p. 63, 98th [actually 97th] Annual Bonspiel Yearbook (1985), p. 35; FP, April 20, 1933, p. 18, April 19, 1934, p. 17, February 10, 1936, p. 12, April 21, 1938, p. 18.

76. FP, February 1, 1933, p. 15, February 6, 1936, p. 14, February 13, 1937, p. 27, February 11, 1938, p. 16, February 16, 1942, p. 19, February 17, 1947, p. 12, February 10, 1948, p. 15; MCA 60th Annual Bonspiel Programme (1948), p. 15, 75th Anniversary Bonspiel Programme (1963), pp. 51-52.

77. MCA 98th [actually 97th] Annual Bonspiel Yearbook (1985), p. 35; FP, January 29, 1952, p. 15, February 2, 1953, p. 19.

78. FP, February 4, 1926, p. 14, February 9, 1926, p. 16, February 10, 1930, p. 9, February 11, 1930, p. 9, February 11, 1936, p. 1, February 12, 1940, p. 16, February 15, 1947, p. 18, February 18, 1947, p. 8, February 15, 1954, p. 18, February 16, 1954, p. 17; Kerr, Curling in Canada and the United States, p. 451; Jean Cochrane, Abby Hoffman and Pat Kincaid, Women in Canadian Sports (Toronto: Fitzhenry and Whiteside Ltd., 1977), chapter 5; interview with Joan Ingram, Winnipeg, September 11, 1987.

79. MCA 75th Anniversary Bonspiel Programme (1963), pp. 104-116, 100th Anniversary Bonspiel Yearbook (1988), pp. 43, 70-74, 78-80, 83-84, 88, 91-94, 97; FP, February 7, 1928, pp. 1, 21, February 11, 1938, p. 16, February 7, 1944, p. 4, November 30, 1946, p. 19, December 4, 1948, p. 19, December 28, 1948, p. 14, February 8, 1954, p. 18, February 3, 1959, p. 19.

80. FP, November 19, 1925, p. 18, April 22, 1926, p. 14, November 18, 1926, p. 20, November 21, 1929, p. 22, November 7, 1939, p. 14, November 16, 1939, p. 19, February 17, 1950, p. 1, November 20, 1952, p. 24, April 16, 1953, p. 26.

81. Numbers of visiting and city rinks are almost always mentioned in press reports on the day the Bonspiel opened. See, for example, FP, February 13, 1939, p. 1, February 7, 1944, p. 1.

82. Ibid., February 5, 1935, p. 1, March 4, 1939, p. 22; MCA 75th Anniversary Bonspiel Programme (1963), p. 60.

83. FP, February 9, 1943, p. 14.

84. Ibid., February 11, 1907, p. 7, February 14, 1913, p. 7, February 6, 1940, p. 12, May 21, 1938, p. 18; interview with Ab Gowanlock, Dauphin, December 21, 1986; MCA *100th Anniversary Bonspiel Yearbook* (1988), p. 59.

85. Henri Bergson, "Laughter," in Wylie Sypher (compiler), *Comedy* (Garden City, New York: Doubleday and Company, Inc., 1956) especially chapter 1.

86. MCA *59th Annual Bonspiel Programme* (1947), p. 41; interviews with Lyle Dyker, Winnipeg, July 3, July 12, 1987, Ab Gowanlock, Dauphin, December 21, 1986, E.R. McKnight, Brandon, June 21, 1987.

87. *FP*, November 19, 1925, p. 18, November 20, 1930, p. 18, November 17, 1932, p. 16, November 16, 1933, p. 18, February 8, 1940, p. 18, April 22, 1948, p. 19.

88. Ibid., April 21, 1932, p. 6, November 17, 1932, p. 16, April 18, 1935, p. 17, April 22, 1948, p. 19, November 18, 1948, p. 20, November 17, 1949, p. 25, November 22, 1951, p. 22; Robert L. Burton (ed.), *A Curling History of Binscarth and Other Stories* (n.p.: R.L. Burton, 1983), p. 29.

89. *FP*, February 4, 1949, p. 16, February 6, 1950, p. 17, February 6, 1951, p. 15, January 28, 1952, p. 14, February 2, 1953, p. 1, February 8, 1954, p. 16, February 7, 1955, p. 16, February 6, 1956, pp. 1, 4, January 28, 1957, p. 1, February 3, 1958, pp. 1, 19, February 2, 1959, p. 19.

90. Ibid., February 7, 1955, p. 16.

CHAPTER 4

1. MCA *100th Anniversary Bonspiel Yearbook* (1988), pp. 165-169; MLCA *Yearbook* (1986-87), pp. 89-95; Murray, *Curling Companion*, pp. 158-162.

2. *FP*, February 21, 1951, p. 18, March 3, 1952, p. 26, March 8, 1967, p. 53, February 23, 1985, p. 53, July 29, 1986, p. 33, July 30, 1986, p. 54; MCA *75th Anniversary Bonspiel Programme* (1963), pp. 54-55, *100th Anniversary Bonspiel Yearbook* (1988), p. 167; MLCA *Yearbook* (1986-87), p. 95; interviews with Cec Watt, Winnipeg, January 25, 1987, C.H. Scrymgeour, Winnipeg, May 26, 1987; transcript of interview of Lyle Dyker by Bob Burton, spring 1987, pp. 7-8, made available by Lyle Dyker.

3. *FP*, March 4, 1959, p. 23, March 5, 1959, p. 29, March 6, 1959, p. 19, March 10, 1960, p. 25, March 27, 1978, p. 35, July 29, 1986, p. 33; interviews with Cec Watt, Winnipeg, January 25, 1987, C.H. Scrymgeour, Winnipeg, May 27, 1987; Smith, *Illustrated History*, p. 163.

4. *FP*, April 7, 1982, p. 51, March 7, 1986, p. 45, April 9, 1987, p. 62; interviews with Cec Watt, Winnipeg,

January 25, 1987, C.H. Scrymgeour, Winnipeg, May 27, 1987, Bob Picken, Winnipeg, July 21, 1987, June 14, 1988, Ina Light, Winnipeg, June 14, 1988.

5. Statistics developed mainly from MCA *100th Anniversary Bonspiel Yearbook* (1988), pp. 164-169, and MLCA *Yearbook* (1986-87), pp. 93-95.

6. Statistics compiled from newspaper reports of results each year.

7. MCA *100th Anniversary Bonspiel Yearbook* (1988), p. 165.

8. *FP*, March 27, 1972, p. 1, April 4, 1972, p. 41; "History of the World Curling Championship," press handout at World Curling Championship, Vancouver, March 30-April 5, 1987, p. 3.

9. *FP*, March 8, 1958, p. 41, March 6, 1965, p. 19, March 19, 1965, p. 43, March 2, 1970, p. 2 of Brier Special, March 7, 1970, p. 57, March 23, 1970, p. 24, March 22, 1971, p. 18; MCA *100th Anniversary Bonspiel Yearbook* (1988), pp. 99-103, 163; interviews with Don Duguid, Winnipeg, July 12, 1987, July 18, 1988, Bryan Wood, Brandon, September 21, 1987.

10. Garry DeBlonde, "Flat Foot or Tuck?," *The Curler*, October 1981, no pages; *FP*, March 4, 1976, p. 47; interviews with Don Duguid, Winnipeg, July 18, 1988, Ray Turnbull, Winnipeg, August 25, 1987, Terry Braunstein, Winnipeg, September 2, 1987, Don Pottinger, Brandon, September 10, 1987.

11. One or more of these reasons are mentioned in *FP*, March 8, 1957, p. 23, March 10, 1961, p. 9, March 6, 1963, p. 32, March 9, 1963, p. 53, March 5, 1969, p. 52, March 8, 1969, p. 54, March 9, 1973, p. 45, March 10, 1973, p. 59; *Trib.*, March 8, 1969, p. 54.

12. Interview with Bryan Wood, Brandon, September 21, 1987; MCA *100th Anniversary Bonspiel Yearbook* (1988), pp. 163-165.

13. *FP*, March 6, 1972, p. 23, March 8, 1972, p. 61, March 5, 1973, p. 26, March 10, 1973, p. 59, March 5, 1977, p. 72, March 12, 1977, p. 72, March 3, 1979, p. 82, March 13, 1989, p. 33, April 10, 1989, pp. 29, 32; *St. John's Evening Telegram*, March 6, 1972, Special Curling Edition, pp. 4A, 5A; *Brandon Sun*, March 6, 1982, "Brier '82," p. 69; Boreham, *The Story of "The Brier,"* "chapter 1979"; MCA *100th Anniversary Bonspiel Yearbook* (1988), p. 163; interview with Jim Ursel, Winnipeg, July 15, 1988.

14. *FP*, March 2, 1970, p. 2 of Brier Special, March 5, 1973, p. 26.

15. *Brandon Sun*, March 11, 1987, p. 8. Similar comments come in the following: *Trib.*, March 4, 1969, p. 18; *FP*, February 13, 1971, p. 51; *Brandon Sun*, March 9, 1982, "Brier '82," p. B2; interview with Don Pottinger, Brandon, September 10, 1987; statement by Rod Hunter, Edmonton, at Manitoba Curling Hall of Fame induction banquet, December 6, 1987.

16. Boreham, *The Story of "The Brier*," "chapter 1958," "chapter 1961," "chapter 1963," "chapter 1974."

17. These reasons are identified in *FP*, March 12, 1963, p. 19, March 5, 1964, p. 41. They were mentioned also in interviews with the following individuals: C.H. Scrymgeour, Winnipeg, June 23, 1987; Terry Braunstein, Winnipeg, July 5, 1987, September 2, 1987; Jimmy Welsh, Winnipeg, July 3, 1987; Lyle Dyker, Winnipeg, July 3, July 12, 1987; Garnet Campbell, Avonlea, Saskatchewan, January 5, 1988.

18. *Trib.*, January 29, 1979, p. 23.

19. *FP*, January 22, 1960, p. 23, March 7, 1964, p. 55; interview with Frank Avery, Vancouver, July 8, 1987.

20. *FP*, February 11, 1937, p. 14, December 9, 1948, p. 21; MCA *65th Annual Bonspiel Programme* (1953), p. 21; *Hamilton Spectator*, March 5, 1949, special Brier section.

21. *FP*, March 27, 1978, p. 36, April 3, 1978, p. 49; Smith, *Illustrated History*, pp. 167-169; Ed Lukowich, Al Hackner and Rick Lang, *Curling to Win* (Toronto: McGraw-Hill Ryerson Ltd., 1986), p. 124; interviews with Ray Turnbull, Winnipeg, February 3, 1987, August 25, 1987; Barbara Huck, "This Broom Sweeps Clean," *Reader's Digest*, January 1988, pp. 129-134; taped interviews conducted in 1987 by Barbara Huck with Otto Danielli and Ray Turnbull. Thanks to Ms. Huck for making available the taped interviews.

22. *FP*, March 11, 1976, p. 55, February 21, 1985, pp. 51, 53, February 23, 1985, p. 62; "C.C.R. and Harper Winners," in Maxwell and Friends, *The First Fifty*, p. 114; Huck, "Spectator Sports Persons," p. 83; interviews with Jack Matheson, Winnipeg, August 25, 1987, Barbara Huck, Winnipeg, June 7, 1988, Don Blanchard, Calgary, August 15, 1988.

23. Matheson, "I'll Take The Brier," "The Brier Builds Character(s)" and "What The Brier Means to Me," in Maxwell and Friends, *The First Fifty*, pp. 44-50, 69-71, 86-87; "C.C.R. and Harper Award Winners," in Maxwell and Friends, *The First Fifty*, p. 114; interviews with Jack Matheson, Winnipeg, August 25, 1987, Barbara Huck, Winnipeg, June 7, 1988.

24. Bill Good, "When the Brier Went Big Time," in Maxwell and Friends, *The First Fifty*, especially p. 45;

interviews with Bob Picken, Winnipeg, June 14, 1988, Bob Irving, Winnipeg, July 18, 1988, Jack Wells, Winnipeg, July 19, 1988.

25. *FP*, April 24, 1964, p. 42, December 8, 1987, p. 46, April 7, 1989, p. 54; MCA *Annual Report*, 1985-86, pp. 8, 21; interviews with Gordon Craig, Toronto, September 15, 1987, Ray Turnbull, Winnipeg, August 25, 1987, Brian Swain, Winnipeg, June 22, 1988, Jack Matheson, Winnipeg, August 25, 1987.

26. Interview with Gordon Craig, Toronto, September 15, 1987; "Behind the Scenes: The CBC Yesterday, In Conversation with Derek Donaldson," in Robert Browning and Don Duguid (eds.), *Championship Curling 1984* (Montreal: CBC Enterprises and Jubillee Productions Canada Ltd., 1984), pp. 101-108.

27. *FP*, March 4, 1952, p. 14, March 6, 1952, p. 21, February 23, 1957, p. 37, February 27, 1970, p. 27.

28. Ibid., March 2, 1970, p. 12, March 4, 1976, p. 61, March 21, 1985, p. 56.

29. This single game attendance record could have been broken easily at the marvellous Saskatoon Brier of 1989. However, the organizers of the event decided to set the capacity of the arena at 8,914. Every draw in Saskatoon drew the same number of people. See the sports pages of the *Regina Leader-Post*, March 6-13, 1989.

30. *FP*, March 3, 1970, p. 22, March 5, 1970, p. 46, March 6, 1970, p. 23, March 7, 1970, p. 57; Boreham, *The Story of "The Brier*," "chapter 1970."

31. *FP*, March 27, 1978, p. 57, March 28, 1978, p. 47, April 3, 1978, p. 51, April 5, 1978, p. 61; interviews with Cec Watt, Winnipeg, January 25, 1987, Bob Picken, Winnipeg, July 21, 1987, Don Turner, Weyburn, September 26, 1987; "History of the World Curling Championship," p. 5.

32. *Brandon Sun*, March 11, 1982, "Brier '82," p. B4, March 16, 1982, p. 6.

33. *FP*, October 20, 1962, p. 51, March 1, 1963, p. 35, March 7, 1963, p. 23, March 5, 1964, p. 41, March 8, 1967, p. 53, March 7, 1968, p. 26, March 27, 1978, p. 36, April 7, 1982, pp. 36, 51; *Trib.*, January 14, 1969, p. 15; MCA *64th Annual Bonspiel Programme* (1952), p. 21; interviews with Cec Watt, Winnipeg, January 25, 1987, Jack Matheson, Winnipeg, August 25, 1987, Bob Picken, Winnipeg, June 14, 1988.

34. *FP*, March 8, 1967, p. 53, January 25, 1978, p. 62; MLCA *Annual Report*, 1967-68, pp. 10, 12-22; resume of career of Lura McLuckie submitted to Manitoba Curling

Hall of Fame, December 1987; interview with Mabel Mitchell, Brandon, July 20, 1988.

35. *FP*, April 29, 1960, p. 51, April 26, 1963, p. 47, April 28, 1967, p. 46, April 24, 1970, p. 50; MCA *Annual Reports*, 1974-75, p. 8, 1979-80, p. 9, 1980-81, p. 13.

36. *FP*, March 2, 1970, Brier Special, p. 12; *Trib.*, February 13, 1946, p. 8; MLCA *Annual Reports*, 1959-60, p. 1, 1965-66, no pages, 1972-73, no pages, 1978-79, no pages, 1985-86, no pages.

37. *FP*, May 13, 1980, p. 72, May 11, 1982, p. 50, October 26, 1985, p. 80, December 21, 1986, p. 32; *Globe and Mail*, December 27, 1986, p. C2; MCA *Annual Reports*, 1979-80, p. 15, 1985-86, p. 9; MCA *Semi-Annual Reports*, 1980, pp. 1, 18, 27, 1982-83, pp. 1, 21, 1983-84, pp. 1, 5, 1985-86, p. 8; Government of Canada, *1984 Tourism and Recreation: A Statistical Digest* (Ottawa: Minister of Supply and Services, Statistics Canada, Education, Culture and Tourism Division, 1984), p. 101; interviews with Cec Watt, Winnipeg, January 25, 1987, July 24, 1988, Patti Vandekerckhove, Winnipeg, January 20, 1987; Results Group, *Report on the Status of Curling in Manitoba*, May 8, 1986, pp. 80-82.

38. MLCA *Yearbook* (1986-87), p. 18.

39. MCA *100th Anniversary Bonspiel Yearbook* (1988), p. 32.

40. *FP*, April 29, 1960, p. 51; MCA *Annual Report*, 1976-77, p. 7, 1985-86, p. 13.

41. MCA *100th Annual Bonspiel Yearbook* (1988), pp. 35-41.

42. MCA *Annual* Report, 1969-70, p. 8; MCA *70th Annual Bonspiel Programme* (1958), pp. 27-30, *100th Anniversary Bonspiel Yearbook* (1988), pp. 35-41.

43. MCA *100th Anniversary Bonspiel Yearbook* (1988), pp. 86, 96; "The Curling Business Heads for a Real Boom," *The Financial Post*, May 23, 1959, p. 39; "Golf Curlers," *The Financial Post*, January 21, 1961, p. R10; "Where the Millions Go in Canada's Golf Boom," *The Financial Post*, January 28, 1961, p. 23; Beatrice Riddell, "Biggest Growth Ever for Golf this Season," *The Financial Post*, April 14, 1962, p. 2.

44. MCA *100th Anniversary Bonspiel Yearbook* (1988), p. 71, *87th Annual Bonspiel Yearbook* (1975), p. 3, *88th Annual Bonspiel Yearbook* (1976), p. 3; PAM, Strathcona Curling Club Collection, introduction to finding aid.

45. *FP*, October 26, 1974, p. 68, October 16, 1975, p. 3; MCA *83rd Annual Bonspiel Yearbook* (1971), p. 3.

46. MCA *71st Annual Bonspiel Programme* (1959), pp. 27-30, *100th Anniversary Bonspiel Yearbook* (1988), pp. 35-41, 95.

47. Artibise, *Winnipeg: An Illustrated History*, pp. 182-189, 205.

48. Interviews with Edna Balderstone and Vince Burr from West St. Paul Club, July 22, 1988.

49. *FP*, April 26, 1968, p. 46, April 27, 1971, p. 58, February 14, 1973, p. 57, April 26, 1973, p. 64, April 26, 1974, p. 48, February 5, 1987, p. 54; MCA *Semi-Annual Report*, 1980-81, p. 1, 1981-82, p. 1; MCA *Annual Report*, 1967-68, p. 2, 1972-73, pp. 6, 19; interviews with Cec Watt, Winnipeg, Jan, 25, 1987, July 24, 1988, Ken Esdale, Winnipeg, August 30, 1988, anonymous City of Winnipeg employee, April 19, 1989.

50. *FP*, April 28, 1967, p. 46; MCA *88th Annual Bonspiel Yearbook* (1976), p. 36; MCA *Annual Report*, 1978-79, p. 8.

51. MLCA *Annual Report*, 1959-60, p. 1; MLCA *Yearbook* (1986-87), p. 21.

52. Interviews with Terry Braunstein, Winnipeg, September 2, 1987, Don Pottinger, Brandon, September 10, 1987, A.G. Bedford, Winnipeg, September 11, 1987, Bob Picken, Winnipeg, June 14, 1988.

53. Elmwood Curling Club, "Club Roster," 1974-75. Thanks to Gary McEwen for making this available. MCA *100th Anniversary Bonspiel Yearbook* (1988), pp. 163-168; MLCA *Yearbook* (1986-87), p. 89.

54. *FP*, January 3, 1988, p. 6. For an indication of the number of Asians, South Americans and others in the city in the 1950s compared to the 1980s, see *Census of Canada*, 1951, table 35, pp. 9-10, *Census of Canada*, 1981, "Population – Manitoba," table 2, pp. 2-3.

55. DeBlonde, "Flat Foot or Tuck?,"n.p.; interviews with Ray Turnbull, Winnipeg, February 3, 1987, August 25, 1987, Don Pottinger, Brandon, September 10, 1987, Terry Braunstein, Winnipeg, July 5, 1987, September 2, 1987, Bob Picken, Winnipeg, June 14, 1988.

56. *FP*, October 19, 1963, p. 55, April 24, 1964, p. 42, April 27, 1967, p. 46, April 28, 1969, p. 23.

57. Curl Canada, Programs and Services (Ottawa: Curl Canada, no date); interviews with Patti Vandekerchhove, Winnipeg, January 20, 1987, A.G. Bedford, Winnipeg, September 11, 1987, C.H. Scrymgeour, Winnipeg, June 23, 1987, Don Duguid, Winnipeg, July 12, 1987, Don Pottinger, Brandon, September 10, 1987, Don Turner, Weyburn, September 26, 1987, Garry DeBlonde, Ottawa,

March 5, 1987; MCA *Annual Reports*, 1978-79, p. 1, 1987-88, pp. 14-18; MCA *100th Anniversary Bonspiel Yearbook* (1988), pp. 163-169.

58. *FP*, March 2, 1970, p. 12, April 2, 1984, p. 37; interviews with Joan Ingram, Winnipeg, September 11, 1987, Ina Light, Winnipeg, June 14, 1988, Chris More (nee Pidzarko), June 14, 1988, Mabel Mitchell, Brandon, July 20, 1988.

59. Interviews with Joan Ingram, Winnipeg, September 11, 1987, Ina Light, Winnipeg, June 14, 1988, Chris More (nee Pidzarko), Winnipeg, June 14, 1988, Mabel Mitchell, Brandon, July 20, 1988; Hoffman, Cochrane and Kincaid, *Women in Canadian Sports*, pp. 63-77; Twin, *Out of the Bleachers: Writings on Women and Sport* (Old Westbury, New York: The Feminist Press, 1979), pp. xv-xli; Paul Phillips, "Women in the Manitoba Labour Market: A Study of the Changing Economic Role," in Henry C. Klassen (ed.), *The Canadian West: Social Change and Economic Development* (Calgary: University of Calgary, 1977), pp. 79-92; Gerald Friesen, "The Prairie West Since 1945: An Historical Survey," in A.W. Rasporich (ed.), *The Making of the Modern West: Western Canada Since 1945* (Calgary: University of Calgary Press, 1984), p. 25.

60. Interviews with C.H. Scrymgeour, Winnipeg, June 23, 1987, A.G. Bedford, Winnipeg, September 11, 1987.

61. MCA *99th Annual Bonspiel Yearbook* (1987), p. 41; *FP*, January 31, 1966, p. 19, April 28, 1966, p. 49, January 30, 1967, p. 23, February 10, 1967, p. 21; *Trib.*, February 6, 1967, p. 13.

62. MCA *99th Annual Bonspiel Yearbook* (1987), p. 41; *FP*, January 30, 1967, p. 23, October 23, 1971, p. 59, January 19, 1988, p. 49; MCA *Annual Report*, 1987-88, pp. 11-12.

63. MCA *78th Annual Bonspiel Programme* (1966), pp. 75, 77, *99th Annual Bonspiel Yearbook* (1987), pp. 71, 73; *FP*, February 15, 1954, p. 18; MCA *Annual Reports*, 1973-74, p. 13, 1975-76, pp. 11-13, 1976-77, p. 11, 1985-86, p. 11.

64. *FP*, February 16, 1954, p. 17; MLCA *Annual Reports*, 1959-60, p. 1, 1962-63, p. 1, 1968-69, p. 1, 1972-73, p. 1, 1976-77, p. 1, 1978-79, p. 1, 1984-85, p. 1.

65. *FP*, January 19, 1988, p. 49.

66. Ibid., January 20, 1975, p. 29, January 23, 1975, p. 50, January 23, 1985, p. 44; MCA *Annual Report*, 1984-85, pp. 1, 8.

67. MCA *100th Annual Bonspiel Yearbook* (1988); p. 57; *FP*, October 20, 1962, p. 51, October 31, 1982, p. 78; MCA *Annual Report*, 1987-88, p. 20C.

68. *FP*, February 3, 1959, p. 19; MCA *75th Annual Bonspiel Programme* (1963), p. 112, *100th Annual Bonspiel Yearbook* (1988), pp. 70, 91.

69. *FP*, January 17, 1987, p. 89.

70. Ibid., February 3, 1959, p. 19, February 1, 1965, p. 19, January 17, 1987, p. 89; MCA *75th Anniversary Bonspiel Programme* (1963), pp. 100-117, *100th Anniversary Bonspiel Yearbook* (1988), pp. 70-97.

71. *FP*, February 8, 1956, p. 20, April 29, 1960, p. 49, April 28, 1961, p. 45, October 20, 1961, p. 43, April 26, 1963, p. 47, April 15, 1965, p. 23, April 22, 1965, p. 41, January 31, 1966, p. 19.

72. Ibid., October 21, 1960, p. 41, April 27, 1962, p. 45, April 22, 1965, p. 41, October 22, 1965, p. 41, January 30, 1967, p. 23, April 26, 1973, p. 64; MCA *Annual Report*, 1974-75, p. 2; interview with Cec Watt, Winnipeg, January 25, 1987.

73. *FP*, October 27, 1975, p. 50, October 20, 1979, p. 94, October 26, 1985, p. 80.

74. For statistics on the decline in the rural population of Manitoba, see Friesen, "The Prairie West Since 1945: An Historical Survey," pp. 14-15.

75. Ibid., pp. 19-23.

76. *FP*, January 17, 1987, p. 89.

77. Morton, *Manitoba*, pp. 480-481; James H. Gray, *Bacchanalia Revisited: Western Canada's Boozy Skid to Social Disaster* (Saskatoon: Western Producer Prairie Books, 1982), chapter 7.

78. MCA *100th Anniversary Bonspiel Yearbook* (1988), pp. 63, 68, 70-97; interviews with Bruce Hudson, Winnipeg, August 25, 1987, Bob Picken, Winnipeg, May 2, 1989.

79. Personal reminiscences of John Allardyce; interviews with Cec Watt, Winnipeg, July 12, 1987, John Frye, Winnipeg, July 14, 1987, Jim Kinnaird, Winnipeg, July 15, 1987.

80. *FP*, February 14, 1916, p. 5, November 22, 1934, p. 19, November 17, 1938, p. 16, April 20, 1939, p. 16.

81. MCA *82nd Annual Bonspiel Programme* (1970), p. 15, *83rd Annual Bonspiel Programme* (1971), p. 15, *84th*

Annual Bonspiel Programme (1972), p. 15; *FP*, April 28, 1972, p. 47.

82. See for example the reports of sermons in *FP*, February 12, 1905, p. 8, February 15, 1909, p. 5, February 17, 1919, p. 5, February 15, 1937, p. 2, February 13, 1950, p. 2.

83. *FP*, October 29, 1977, p. 75.

84. Conversations with several curlers in Fairbanks, Alaska, November 5-12, 1987, and Lausanne, Switzerland, April 9-16, 1988.

CONCLUSION

1. *FP*, February 6, 1965, p. 56, March 4, 1965, p. 42, February 10, 1967, p. 21, March 3, 1971, p. 31, April 27, 1971, p. 58, March 10, 1972, p. 41; MCA *Annual Report*, 1971-72, pp. 2, 18.

2. *FP*, April 26, 1973, p. 64, October 27, 1973, p. 65, March 3, 1980, p. 45, March 7, 1980, p. 55, October 16, 1981, p. 54; MCA *Annual Report*, 1972-73, p. 38, 1973-74, 39-40, 1974-75, p. 38, 1979-80, pp. 2, 30; interviews with Cec Watt, Winnipeg, January 25, 1987, Bob Picken, Winnipeg, July 21, 1987.

3. *FP* March 7, 1980, p. 55, October 22, 1983, p. 90, March 7, 1985, pp. 45-46, December 6, 1987, p. 26; MCA *Semi-Annual Report*, 1981-82, pp. 1-3, 1983-84, pp. 3-11; MCA *Annual Report*, 1983-84, pp. 8, 31, 1984-85, pp. 2, 6; interviews with Cec Watt, Winnipeg, January 25, 1987, Bob Picken, Winnipeg, July 21, 1987, Noel Buxton, Winnipeg, May 27, 1987.

4. *FP*, October 25, 1986, p. 87, December 6, 1987, p. 26, December 28, 1988, p. 34; interviews with Cec Watt, Winnipeg, January 25, 1987, Bob Picken, Winnipeg, July 21, 1987.

Glossary

CURLING TERMS USED IN THIS VOLUME

"A" group: The best teams in a curling club. Clubs normally arrange to have teams of roughly equal calibre play against each other regularly. "A" group teams will have the best players, then there will be "B" group teams, and so on.

Air Canada Silver Broom: The men's world championship event from 1968 through 1985.

Arras: The running surface around the concave bottom of the rock.

Artificial ice: Ice made on top of a floor that is artificially cooled, usually by means of a cold brine flowing through pipes buried just below the floor.

Back-ring weight: Weight sufficient to take a rock to the back of the house.

Biter: A rock partially in the twelve-foot circle.

Blank end: An end in which no points are counted.

Bonspiel: A curling tournament, usually involving a number of events. The MCA's Annual Bonspiel has been consistently the biggest annual bonspiel in the world.

Borrow: See the second entry under "ice."

British Consols: The Manitoba men's championship event from 1925 through 1979.

Broom: A tool used to sweep a rock in order to make the rock travel further and straighter than it would when left on its own. The brooms are of two types: the straw broom, or corn broom, which has a head made of straw or corn and is used with a slapping motion; the push broom, which has a head made of horse hair or hog hair and is used with a brushing motion. The term "the broom" also refers to the broom held by the skip or third as a target for the thrower.

Burned rock: A rock touched inadvertently by a curler.

Button: The smallest circle in the house, at the centre of the house, usually one foot in diameter.

Calcutta: An auction of teams in a bonspiel, with paybacks based on results.

Canadian Curling Association (CCA): The national administrative organization for men's curling. It was known as the Dominion Curling Association (DCA) from 1935 to 1968.

Canadian Ladies' Curling Association (CLCA): The national administrative organization for women's curling, established in 1961.

Club: (1) An association of curlers. (2) A curling facility.

Crampits: Portable bases, normally made of iron, that were used to enable a curler to gain a foothold on the ice when throwing a rock. Replaced over time by hacks.

Curl: (1) The act of playing the game of curling. (2) The action of a thrown rock – it curls, or curves, across the sheet of ice.

Delivery: The physical act of putting a rock in motion.

Double take-out: The removal of two opposition rocks with one throw.

Down: Trailing in a game; that is, having a lower score.

Draw: (1) A schedule of competition. (2) The movement across the ice by a rock (see the second entry under "curl"). (3) A shot coming to rest in the house.

Draw game: A strategy of play featuring draws and other shots involving quiet weight.

Draw weight: Weight sufficient to take a rock into the house.

End: A distinct segment of a game in which each team plays eight shots. At present, ten ends constitute a game. An "extra end" is a sudden-death end played in the event of a tie after the regular number of ends.

Event: A specific competition, usually used when referring to bonspiels, which are composed of several events. An "open event" is one that any team can enter. A "closed event" is one for which teams must qualify.

Fall: A section of a sheet of ice where a rock will move in the direction opposite the turn imparted.

Flat-foot delivery: A type of sliding delivery in which the weight of the body rests primarily on the sole of the sliding (front) foot, and in which the legs do not touch each other.

Front end: The lead and second on a team.

Grand Aggregate: The trophy awarded to the team with the best record in the major events of a bonspiel, particularly the MCA Bonspiel.

Grand Match: An annual bonspiel held on a lake in Scotland chosen for the event. The Grand Match originated in 1847; over the years many grand matches have had to be cancelled because of weather.

Guard: (1) A rock situated in front of another, making it difficult for the opposition to take out the latter stone. (2) A type of shot in which the purpose is to put the rock in front of the house in order to protect a rock that either is in the house, or will be once later shots are played.

Hack: A hole in the ice, normally with a rubber insert, used by the curler as a foothold when throwing a rock. There are two hacks at each end of the rink, one used by left-handers, the other by right-handers.

Hack weight: Weight sufficient to move an opposition rock back to the hacks.

Heavy ice: A sheet of ice that requires fast throws for rocks to reach the rings.

Hit: A shot that removes an opponent's stone from play, or at least moves it out of a scoring position.

Hog-lines: Two lines across the sheet, each thirty-three feet from the near hack. The lines are seventy-two feet apart. A rock must pass the far hog-line to be in play. In recent years, a curler throwing a rock must release it before reaching the near hog-line.

Home end: Playing toward the clubhouse. "Coming home" means playing the last end.

House: A series of four concentric circles at either end of the sheet. The centre point of each of the concentric circles is twelve feet from the near hacks. The house is the target at which curlers throw their rocks. Since 1903 (in Manitoba) the circles have been one foot (the "button"), four feet, eight feet and twelve feet in diameter.

Ice: (1) The surface of play, usually referred to as a "sheet of ice," now 146 feet long and fourteen feet two inches wide. (2) The amount of "curl" or "borrow" allowed for when playing a shot. If two feet of ice is "taken," then the curler expects the rock to move two feet across the ice while it goes from delivery point to stopping point.

International Curling Federation (ICF): The administrative organization for international curling, founded in 1966.

In-turn: The turn applied to a rock by a player who turns the elbow in at release. In-turns thrown by a left-handed player turn counter-clockwise; those thrown by a right-handed player turn clockwise.

Irons: Curling rocks made of iron, used very infrequently (in Manitoba) after the 1890s.

Keen ice: A sheet of ice that allows slowly thrown rocks to reach the other end.

Knock-out game: A strategy of play which emphasizes take-outs instead of draws.

Labatt Brier: The Canadian men's championship event from 1980 to the present.

Labatt Tankard: The Manitoba men's championship event from 1980 to the present.

Lead: The player who throws the first two rocks (first pair) for the team.

MacDonald Brier: The Canadian men's championship event from 1927 through 1979.

Manitoba Curling Association (MCA): The provincial administrative organization for men's curling. Formed in 1888 as the Manitoba Branch, Royal Caledonian Curling Club of Edinburgh, Scotland. The name was changed in 1908.

Manitoba Ladies' Curling Association (MLCA): The provincial administrative organization for women's curling. Formed in 1925.

Middle score: A line drawn across the middle of the ice in the early years of curling. The middle score was sixty-nine feet from the hacks at either end.

Mixed rink: A team composed of both women and men, usually two of each, throwing in alternate order.

Out-turn: The turn applied to a rock by a player who turns the elbow out at release. Out-turns thrown by a left-hander turn clockwise; those thrown by a right-hander turn counter-clockwise.

Pebble: The pebble is the frozen droplets of water sprayed on the ice before a game, providing a surface on which the rock slides and curls.

Percentage: A statistical measure of a player's or team's performance.

Points competition: A competition especially prominent in curling's early days. It required individual curlers to attempt a series of shots without help from sweepers. Points were awarded for the degree of success with which each shot was made, and the total scores determined the winner.

Raise: A type of shot that moves another rock forward. Usually the rock that has been hit moves into the house, but sometimes it knocks another rock out of the house. A player attempting this latter shot would be playing a "raise take-out."

Read the ice: Determine the amount of weight and curl required to make different shots in all parts of the sheet.

Rings: See "house."

Rink: (1) A physical structure housing one or more sheets of ice. (2) A team of curlers.

Roarin' game: An affectionate term for curling. Probably derived from the sound of rocks travelling down a sheet of ice.

Rock: The object of play in curling, like the puck in hockey or the ball in baseball. Usually made out of polished granite, but formerly sometimes made of wood or iron.

Roll: The path a rock takes after it strikes a stationary rock at an angle.

Royal Caledonian Curling Club (RCCC): The administrative body of curling in Scotland. Affectionately referred to as the "mother club," though it is in fact an association of clubs.

Run: (1) A section of the sheet where rocks move straight ahead rather than curl. (2) To remove a guard; that is, the lead might attempt to run the opposition's guard.

Running game: A knock-out game, with the connotation of comparatively heavy weight.

Running weight: Strong weight.

Scotch Cup: The forerunner of the official men's world championship. The Scotch Cup was played from 1959 through 1967.

Second: The player who throws the third and fourth rocks (the second pair) for the team.

Shot: A throw.

Shot rock: The rock in the house closest to the centre of the rings.

Skip: The player who directs play for the team and usually throws the seventh and eighth rocks (the final pair).

Slide: What a player does while making a "delivery."

Stone: See "rock."

Sweeping: Motion made with a broom in front of a moving rock. "Sweepers" are the two members of a team who are neither holding the broom at one end nor throwing the rock at the other. The "lead" and "second" do more sweeping than the "third" or "skip" do.

Take-out: See "hit."

Take-out game: See "knock-out game."

Tee-line: A line across the sheet at either end, each twelve feet from the near hacks, and running through the mid-point of the house.

Third: The player who throws the fifth and sixth rocks (third pair) for the team, and who normally directs play when the "skip" plays his or her shots.

Tuck delivery: A type of sliding delivery in which the weight of the body rests primarily on the toes of the sliding (front) foot, and in which the heel of the sliding foot rests on the opposite thigh.

Turn: The direction in which the handle of the rock is turned, usually referred to as "in-turn" or "out-turn."

Up: Leading in a game; that is, being ahead on the scoreboard.

Weight: The speed of a thrown rock, usually referred to in terms such as "heavy" or "draw."

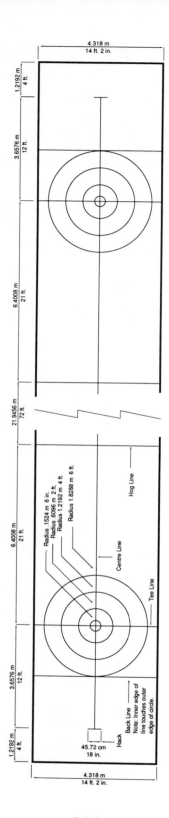

4.318 m
14 ft. 2 in.

1.2192 m
4 ft.

3.6576 m
12 ft.

6.4008 m
21 ft.

21.9456 m
72 ft.

6.4008 m
21 ft.

Radius .1524 m 6 in.
Radius .6096 m 2 ft.
Radius 1.2192 m 4 ft.
Radius 1.8288 m 6 ft.

Centre Line

Hog Line

Tee Line

3.6576 m
12 ft.

Back Line
Note: Inner edge of
line touches outer
edge of circle.

Hack

1.2192 m
4 ft.

45.72 cm
18 in.

4.318 m
14 ft. 2 in.

Index